LITTLE CROW

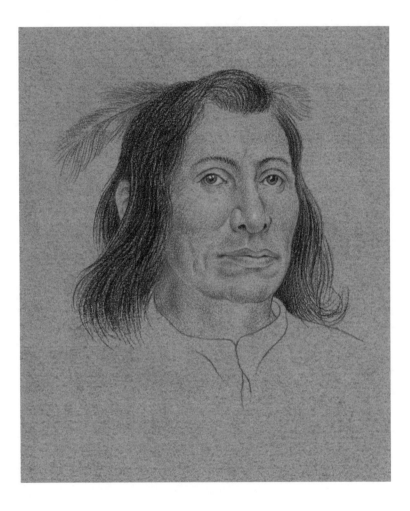

LITTLE CROW

T A O Y A T E D U T A

◀◀ Leader of the Dakota ▶▶

GWENYTH SWAIN

BOREALIS BOOKS

S

Borealis Books is an imprint of the Minnesota Historical Society Press.
www.borealisbooks.org

The Minnesota Historical Society Press is a member of the
Association of American University Presses.

Manufactured in the United States of America

10 9 8 7 6 5 4 3 2 1

♾ The paper used in this publication meets the minimum requirements of
the American National Standard for Information Sciences—Permanence for
Printed Library Materials, ANSI Z39.48-1984.

International Standard Book Number 0-87351-502-1 (cloth)
0-87351-503-X (paper)

Library of Congress Cataloging-in-Publication Data

Swain, Gwenyth, 1961–
Little Crow : leader of the Dakota / Gwenyth Swain.
p. cm.
Includes bibliographical references and index.
ISBN 0-87351-502-1 (hardcover : alk. paper)
ISBN 0-87351-503-X (pbk. : alk. paper)
1. Little Crow, d. 1863. 2. Dakota Indians—Kings and rulers—Biography.
3. Dakota Indians—Wars, 1862-1865. I. Title: At head of title: Taoyateduta. II. Title.

E99.D1L733 2004
978.004'975243'0092—dc22
2003019913

Now what have we? Why, we have neither our lands, where our fathers' bones are bleaching, nor have we anything. What shall we do?

LITTLE CROW/TAOYATEDUTA, 1852

TABLE OF CONTENTS

ACKNOWLEDGMENTS

THE AUTHOR wishes to acknowledge the contributions of many individuals and organizations to this book.

For their willingness to read and comment on the manuscript in progress, I thank the following members of the Dakota community, descendants of Taoyateduta: Dr. Elden Lawrence, Reverend Floyd Heminger, and LeeAnn TallBear. All tried to help me understand traditions and concepts that for a non-Dakota are difficult to grasp. Any misrepresentations of Dakota life that remain in this book after their help reflect only my failure to understand.

For their helpful comments on the manuscript in progress and for generous sharing of expertise on historical and other topics, I thank the following individuals: Laura L. Anderson, University of Oklahoma; Marcia Marshall; Shannon Pennefeather; Sally Rubinstein; Thomas Shaw, Historic Fort Snelling; and Tim Talbott and Dan Fjeld, Lower Sioux Agency Historic Site.

For research assistance, I acknowledge the following people and places: Tim Glines, Minnesota Historical Society; the reference staff of the Minnesota Historical Society library; the staffs of the Lower Sioux Agency Historic Site and Fort Ridgely; and Alan Woolworth.

For their support of this project from its inception, particular thanks go to the staff of Borealis Books and to Debbie Miller.

And many thanks to my husband, Vince Dolan.

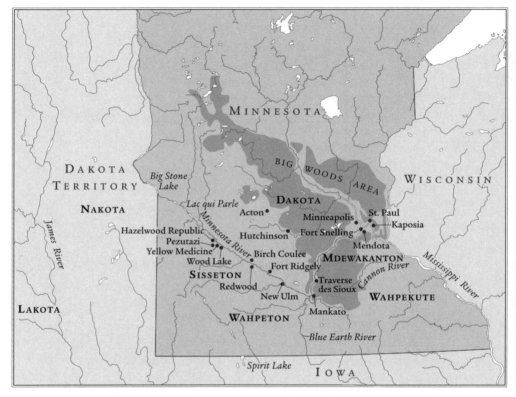

Map of the Upper Midwest circa 1862, showing five major groups of
the Dakota nation.

LITTLE CROW

INTRODUCTION

DIFFERENT CULTURES often have different names for the very same things. The village the Dakota Indians called Kaposia is now part of a place white people named South St. Paul, Minnesota. Sometime around 1810 a Dakota baby was born at Kaposia. White people in Minnesota called him Little Crow—when they weren't calling him the devil or other names just as bad. "Little Crow" wasn't his name at all, but a poor translation into French and then into English of his grandfather's name, *Cetanwakanmani*, which means "Charging Hawk" in the Dakota language.

Canoes float on the Mississippi River near a Dakota village, most likely Kaposia, in about 1846. Painting by Seth Eastman.

The boy's mother probably gave him his first name. When she held him in her arms, she would have called him *Chaska* (first-born son) or *Michinkshi* (my son). But she knew he was destined for great things and would certainly earn a different name by the time he was a man. It was no great surprise, then, when he was named *Ta-o-ya-te-du-ta*. In English *Taoyateduta* means "His Red Nation." It was the kind of name one might give to a leader.

For many years, Taoyateduta was impatient to live up to his name. In the end, however, his name seemed to mock him. Taoyateduta became the leader of a war that scattered the Dakota people across the prairies, forcing most of them to leave their homeland, Minnesota, far behind. By 1862, his red nation—the Dakota nation—was deeply divided. And the life Taoyateduta had known seemed to be dissolving into the golden prairie sunset.

CHAPTER 1

A Dakota Boy

The half-grown boys & the dogs of the Indian village are the greatest
pests it has been my fortune to meet. . . . Very dirty, very ugly & very
mischievous.   FRANK MAYER, 1851

They told me that their nation had always lived in the valley of the
Mississippi—that their wise men had asserted this for ages past.

MARY EASTMAN, 1849

WHEN THE BOY called Chaska was born, his family lived on the
eastern shore of the Mississippi River, just south of present-day
St. Paul, Minnesota. It's likely he was born there in the village of
Kaposia. Kaposia was where his family stayed the longest in any
given year. It was where the women planted corn in summer and
where they lived in lodges made from tree bark. The name *Kaposia*
means "traveling light," and the people were often on the move.
They were always looking for good places to hunt for deer or gather
food like the wild rice that grew in Minnesota lakes.

When Chaska was very young, he traveled in a diaper of soft
deerskin lined with the fuzz of a cattail. His mother carried him

over her back in a cradleboard, a kind of backpack with a rigid wooden frame. When she gathered wood, she might prop the cradleboard against a tree trunk or hang it from a grapevine so Chaska could entertain himself by watching the birds.

When the whole village picked up and moved to their fall and winter hunting grounds along the St. Croix River, Chaska's cradleboard was hung along the side of a horse, a bundle of blankets on the other side to balance the load. As he grew older, he saw the trail to northern lakes from the top of a fully loaded travois, a

Alexander Hesler took this photograph of St. Anthony Falls in 1851 looking west from Hennepin Island to the future site of Minneapolis. Like many early visitors to the area, Hesler was impressed by the awesome power of the falls— and the industries it might someday help run. He and others like him tended to send back east images of the area's natural resources rather than images of its people, the Dakota, who had called the region home for generations.

kind of sled made from long wooden poles and harnessed to a pack animal, sometimes a dog. As long as that animal kept to the trail, Chaska had an easy ride. But every so often, at the whiff of a fox or a rabbit, a dog might pull a travois deep into the woods.

During those early travels in a cradleboard, on a travois, or on foot, Chaska came to know the cycles of the year. Throughout all the moons, or Dakota months, Chaska and his family traveled from place to place. They looked for spots to camp with plenty of food and firewood nearby. Late in fall, in *Takiyuha wi,* the moon when deer mated, they left Kaposia and headed north, searching for deer tracks in the snow. Men hunted for deer and other game while women put up elk- or buffalo-skin tepees and made them snug against the cold whistling winds of *Tahcapsun wi,* the moon when bucks lost their horns and the midday sun shone feebly.

In the hard moon of *Witehi wi,* when the deer were so thin that they were hardly worth hunting, Chaska's people headed back to a spot near Kaposia. They dug up corn or rice sealed in bark barrels and stored in shallow holes at the village. They fished in the river through holes in the ice. And together they waited through the worst of the winter.

As long as the fall hunt had been successful and there was plenty to eat, the Kaposia band could look forward to a comfortable late winter and spring. Chaska watched men fix traps for muskrats and make shot for their hunting guns. He watched women scrape and smoke deer hides until they were soft and supple yet strong. And during *Istawicayazan wi,* the moon of sore eyes, when winds blasted down and kept the smoke from the wood fire inside his

Indian Sugar Camp, 1853. Engraving after sketch by Seth Eastman.

family's tepee, he listened to stories of past hunts and past winters spent along the rivers and woods and hills.

When spring finally came, in the month of *Watopapi wi,* when the rivers and streams were free of ice, Chaska helped his father and uncles and older cousins. They were getting ready for the long trip west to the lakes where muskrats lived. Chaska was too young to go along. Instead, he joined the women going to the sugar bush, a place where many maple trees grew. Boys and girls and women worked together at the sugar bush to gather sap from the trees and boil it down to thick, golden-brown sugar. Women and girls tapped the trees and gathered wood for the fires. Boys like Chaska guarded the syrup as it turned into sugar and fought off hungry chipmunks, rabbits, and squirrels.

A DAKOTA BOY

Most of the men hunted with guns or spears, but Chaska and the other boys stalked their prey with old-fashioned bows and arrows. Chaska had probably owned his set since he was old enough to hold it in his hands. Days and months and years of practice made Dakota boys good shots.

After preparing the maple sugar, everyone headed home to Kaposia, where the men would soon join them, their packs piled high with muskrat pelts. As soon as the wild strawberries turned red, during the month *Wozupi wi,* Chaska's mother and the other women of Kaposia started planting corn.

Among the Dakota, farming was women's work. But boys were expected to help in the fields, especially late in summer when red-winged blackbirds tried to peck at the ripening ears of corn. The boys helped their mothers and grandmothers build wooden platforms in the fields. Then they sat on top to keep watch for flocks of blackbirds, letting out cries and whoops when the birds tried to come near the corn. On lazy summer days, between blackbird attacks, Chaska dozed in the heat of *Wazustecasa wi,* the month for hoeing corn, and listened to stories his mother or grandmother—sitting below in the shade of the platform—might tell.

Once they had gathered the ripe corn during the month of *Wasuton wi,* Chaska and his people prepared for fall. Women and children headed north to lakes where wild rice and cranberries grew. In *Wazupi wi,* the moon for drying rice, they worked together to preserve the harvest for winter.

Soon the men headed out again for the fall deer hunt. All day long, Chaska waited for the hunters to return to camp. He hoped

"A scaffold, six or seven feet high, is raised in the field, and there the women and children sit, watching through the long day. . . . Children are glad to be called upon; for while they sit under the robe which forms a kind of awning, they can dance, or talk and laugh, or what is still better, listen to long, miraculous stories about beavers or bears that have souls like men, or about great black spiders that have journeyed all over the world." Mary Eastman, 1853

to be the first to catch sight of them, so he could call out "Woo-coo-hoo!" That call let everyone know that freshly killed deer was on its way. There would be feasting that night. If a lucky hunter brought a bear, Chaska shouted "Wah! wah! wah!" Chaska and the other boys kept shouting and hollering until all the hunters had returned.

Dakota men were great hunters. They had to be if their people were to have plenty to eat and deerskin to fashion into warm buckskin moccasins. Chaska only had to feel hungry for a few days during a bad hunt to realize that he wanted to be a great hunter, too. In the early 1800s, the land around Chaska's home was full of squirrels, chipmunks, red fox, rabbits, and deer. Rivers and streams were teeming with walleyed pike. Learning to track deer on foot or to spear fish through river ice might be hard work, but Dakota boys made it seem like a game.

Each trip into the woods revealed new secrets of the natural world. Armed with a bow and arrow for hunting and a pole with a horsehair line for fishing, Chaska walked lightly, observing everything around him. The leaves that were disturbed around a particular tree showed that a deer had made its bed there, or perhaps a bear had been scratching for roots. Chaska didn't always know what the clues meant, but his searching taught him about the animals of the forest, how they lived and slept, and how a good hunter might track them.

When Chaska saw rabbit tracks in the morning grass, he scattered piles of sharply pointed burrs on the ground. The next morning he hoped to find a sad-looking rabbit stopped by burrs stuck in its feet. If this didn't work, he gathered his burrs and tried again.

Older relatives helped Chaska when he needed it. One taught him how to make bows and arrows. Another shared his skill in shooting. Still others helped Chaska memorize the habits and ways of animals. Being a good hunter meant more than knowing how to shoot. It meant being so close to nature that you *knew*, deep down, where animals gathered.

Stories told around the nighttime fire helped Chaska understand that even animals like the wolf, or *shunktokeca,* had much to teach him. A wise father would tell his son, "follow the example of the shunktokeca. . . . Even when he is surprised and runs for his life, he will pause to take one more look at you before he enters his final retreat. So you must take a second look at everything you see."

Chaska also had to be brave, and he had to know how to force his body to survive long, hard days of hunting. Most likely his father, *Wakinyantanka* (Big Thunder), was his first teacher. Early in the morning, Wakinyantanka might rouse Chaska from his sleep and challenge him to fast for the day. Chaska needed to know how to maintain his strength without food if someday he was to join the men hunting. Fasting would help make him brave, especially since he had to endure the taunts of the other boys at Kaposia, as they grabbed tasty bits of stew and ate right in front of him.

But Chaska didn't let the taunting get to him. He taunted them right back on their fasting days. And he joined their games on days when learning to hunt seemed less important than testing a sled on a snow-covered hill. In winter, when the cold deepened, Dakota boys built sleds from long, narrow strips of bark. Boys challenged each other to go down the steepest, most tree-covered hills. They skated the rivers, too, wearing smaller strips of bark tied to their moccasined feet.

Skating was fun and safe as long as the ice held, but when the sun began to shine more strongly in the spring, river and lake ice started to crack and boom. One year, on a late winter day, a boy fell through the ice into cold, cold water. Chaska tied one end of

A Dakota Boy

Detail from *Spearing Muskrats in Winter,* 1853.
Engraving after sketch by Seth Eastman.

a pack line to a tree on the shore and threw the other to his friend. Then, when it seemed the river water might still pull the boy under, Chaska jumped in and pulled the boy to shore. Although still young, Chaska was earning a reputation for bravery and strength. He hoped to make his father and his village proud of him. But sometimes it seemed as though he didn't belong at Kaposia.

Chaska's mother, *Miniokadawin* (Woman Planting in Water), came from Wabasha's village, far down the Mississippi River. Men from Kaposia often chose wives from other villages and brought them to Kaposia, but Chaska's mother didn't stay. When Chaska was still young, she went back to her own people. Since then, Wakinyan-tanka had married again, and Chaska was surrounded by much younger half-brothers and -sisters. They made a bark lodge feel crowded and were too little to be much fun to play with.

But even if he felt out of place, Chaska didn't ignore his relatives. No one could and still be Dakota. In a Dakota village, nearly everyone was related. Chaska had many fathers, since the Dakota considered all of his father's brothers to be his father, too. All of his mother's sisters were also mothers to him. Children whom white visitors would have called Chaska's cousins he naturally called his brothers and sisters. Chaska's family extended well beyond the cozy lodge he shared with his grandparents and parents and brothers and sisters. Everywhere he went, Chaska found relatives. If he were to meet someone, like a white man, who wasn't somehow related, he could still make him part of the family by claiming him as a brother or a cousin.

The Dakota had always viewed family this way. They trusted that family would see them through hard times. Grandparents, who were often children's first teachers, told young hunters like Chaska, "Give food! Give food unstintingly! Let nothing be held in reserve for one alone. When all food is gone, then we shall honorably starve together. Let us still be Dakotas!" So Chaska learned to share the rabbits he trapped and the fish he caught. In the Dakota way of thinking, everything he gave away would eventually flow back to him. The Dakota way of life depended on family and relatives caring for each other.

In many ways, Chaska was just one of many sons or brothers at Kaposia. But in other ways, he was special. He was the oldest grandson of the leader Cetanwakanmani. After Chaska's father,

A Dakota Boy

A view of a Dakota village on the Mississippi, most likely Kaposia,
from circa 1846, by Seth Eastman.

Wakinyantanka, had his time as leader, Chaska expected to become
leader himself. As leader, he wouldn't live in a better lodge or tepee.
Dakota leaders didn't eat better than others in the village. And
they didn't have better horses or clothes. Their power didn't come
from the things they had but often from the things they gave
away. Cetanwakanmani gained power by making sure that all in
the village had enough to eat and warm shelter for winter. He
gained influence by being good to relatives—and by being good to
the village.

As leader, Chaska's grandfather knew how to listen well. The
Dakota made their decisions together, in meetings called councils.
Over hours or days or weeks, they met to discuss major decisions.
The leader did his best to listen to and sort through all the different

views. His job was to make clear the decisions his people had reached, not to tell people what to do.

About the time that Chaska's grandfather became leader of the Kaposia band, Dakota leaders began to take on a new role. White people were moving into Dakota lands. Some were French speaking, and many more were English speaking. The Dakota called them *Wasicu*. The name didn't mean "white" exactly, but referred to beings who were very efficient and had odd, almost magical, powers.

The Wasicu didn't see the point in spending hours and days in council when one man could make a good decision quickly and efficiently. They came to village leaders whenever they had something important to discuss. The first Wasicu with something important to discuss with Cetanwakanmani was Lieutenant Zebulon Montgomery Pike of the United States Army. He came to Kaposia on September 23, 1805, a few years before Chaska was born.

Pike was looking for land on which to build a frontier fort. Not far from Kaposia, he found what he wanted. For about one hundred thousand acres of land, Pike paid Cetanwakanmani and another leader two hundred and fifty dollars in gifts, which they promptly gave to their villages. Cetanwakanmani didn't think of land the way this Wasicu Pike did—as something to be bought and sold. He did not know that Pike told other whites he'd gotten the land "for a song."

Cetanwakanmani would not have agreed to Pike's fort if he hadn't believed that the people of Kaposia would welcome it. But Cetanwakanmani did not understand what changes white people would bring. At first, when Chaska was very young, little changed around Kaposia. People hunted and fished and gathered wild rice as they always had. In good years, they sold furs to traders. In bad years, they went hungry together.

It wasn't until 1817, when Chaska was about seven years old, that another group of Wasicu came up the Mississippi River to talk again about the fort. In July, Major Stephen Long and his men rowed past the burial ground for Kaposia's dead on the west bank of the Mississippi and then past the village to the east. Long didn't spend much time in the area. But he did choose a site on a high bluff overlooking the place where the Minnesota and Mississippi Rivers come together. Two years later, a bigger group arrived, ready at last to build the frontier fort.

Major Thomas Forsyth, a gray-haired man who had spent much of his life working with Indians, was sent to talk with the Dakota. It was late July by the time he arrived at Kaposia. Chaska was probably there when Forsyth met Cetanwakanmani. Forsyth reported that Cetanwakanmani was "a steady, generous and independent Indian."

We don't know what Chaska or Cetanwakanmani thought of Forsyth, but we do know what Forsyth told the Dakota. The president of the United States—the Great Father—had sent him and the troops. The Dakota, or Sioux, he assured them, "must not think that anything bad was intended; . . . a fort . . . would answer two purposes for the Sioux—first, it would be a place that any little thing they might want repaired by the blacksmith would be done for them, and also be a place of trade; secondly, their enemies would not be allowed to injure any of the Sioux Indians at or near the fort." Forsyth handed out gifts to Cetanwakanmani and other leaders along the Mississippi and Minnesota Rivers. But because he liked Cetanwakanmani so much, and because Kaposia was the village closest to the new fort, Forsyth gave the biggest gifts to Chaska's people.

Forsyth's report on the Dakota probably impressed Major Lawrence Taliaferro [TAHL-uh-ver], who arrived at the fort that same year, in 1819. Taliaferro was the new Indian agent. He was supposed to explain to Dakota leaders the policies of the U.S. government. And he was to try to keep the peace between the Dakota and their new Wasicu neighbors. He also hoped to bring about a peace between the Dakota and their long-time enemies to the north, the Ojibwe. Young men and boys like Chaska dreamed of proving their bravery and skill as warriors by fighting the Ojibwe. But the U.S. government wanted peace on Indian lands.

Taliaferro never stopped the Dakota and Ojibwe from fighting, but he did keep the whites around the fort and their Dakota neighbors from shooting each other. He was proud to take credit for this, but Taliaferro's success depended on leaders like Cetanwakanmani.

Chaska's grandfather liked the Indian agent, even though this Wasicu had a way of thinking too much of himself. The leader, his son, and Chaska often visited Taliaferro at his house just outside the stone walls of the new fort. Cetanwakanmani never left the agent's house without first saying, "My father I take you by the hand." And he rarely left without first having a drink of whiskey.

Chaska knew about the Wasicu drink, whiskey, long before he

A DAKOTA BOY

met Taliaferro. The same traders who sold the Dakota blankets and guns also sold them *minnewakan,* or "spirit water," as the Dakota sometimes called the drink. When Dakota boys played white man—using white clay to paint their faces and moss for beards—they always had water on hand to stand in for whiskey. Chaska traded furs for sips of water, for bags of "sugar" that looked more like sand, and for ground-up earth that was meant to look like gunpowder.

Lawrence Taliaferro was Indian agent at Fort Snelling beginning in 1819. His job was to keep peace between the Dakota and the Ojibwe and to teach them how to farm.

But real minnewakan was no game. In more than one Dakota village, men had to tie drunken warriors to the poles of a lodge at night to keep them from destroying things as they roared around in the dark. By the time Chaska was a teenager, even Cetanwakan-mani was drinking more than he should.

Perhaps in part because of the leader's drinking, people began to leave Kaposia for other villages in the 1820s. The deer and other game that had been so plentiful in years past seemed to be hiding somewhere in the Big Woods to the west. Kaposia's hunters—and hunters in other Dakota villages—were finding it harder to find game to kill for food and furs. At the same time, local traders were raising prices on goods at their stores.

It couldn't have been easy for Chaska to watch his village grow smaller and smaller over the years. It couldn't have been easy to watch his own grandfather stumble around drunk. It couldn't have been easy to feel hunger in his stomach when he and other hunters failed to find enough game to carry the families through the winter.

Sometime in the late 1820s or early 1830s, Chaska earned a new name, a name fit for a man—*Ta-o-ya-te-du-ta*. "His Red Nation" was a good name for a leader of a people, but Taoyateduta wasn't sure that Kaposia was a good place to lead from. It seemed as if the villagers were scattering far and wide through the woods. What chance was there here to find glory, respect, or power? Taoyateduta decided to follow the others, leaving his village and his people behind.

CHAPTER 2

Searching and Traveling

The village at Lac-qui-parle consisted of about 400 persons, chiefly of the Wahpaton, or Leaf-village band of the Dakotas. They were very poor and very proud.

STEPHEN R. RIGGS, 1880

AT FIRST when Taoyateduta left his village, he had his father's and his grandfather's approval. When Wakinyantanka or Cetan-wakanmani wanted to send a message to a nearby village, they gave Taoyateduta the job. He might take a dugout canoe up the Minnesota River to Shakopee's village. Or he might float down the muddy green Mississippi to Lake Pepin and Wabasha's village beyond.

Wherever he went, Taoyateduta brought more than just his grandfather's or his father's words. He brought news of the fort, growing bigger each year on the bluff where the two rivers met. He brought news of the Wasicu with their guns and endless supplies of food. He told about great boats that belched steam and made their way upriver without a single paddlestroke. More of these steamboats were riding up the Mississippi River each year.

21

While serving as a messenger or while hunting, Taoyateduta traveled throughout his people's lands. His people were the Mdewakanton Dakota of the woods around the lower St. Croix, Mississippi, and Minnesota Rivers. They were one of seven groups that made up a great Indian nation, which the Wasicu called the Sioux. Taoyateduta and other eastern members of this nation called themselves Dakota. Their western neighbors called themselves Nakota or Lakota. Along with the Mdewakanton, there were the Sissetons, who gathered mainly near Big Stone Lake, many miles west of Kaposia. There were the Wahpetons, who built their lodges closer by, along the Minnesota River. Then there were the Wahpekutes, who lived near the Blue Earth and Cannon Rivers.

Taoyateduta probably met Yankton and Yanktonai Nakota while traveling to the James River to trade for buffalo hides. He may not have met any of the even more distant Lakota, the Tetons, who rode their ponies over the Great Plains in what is now North and South Dakota. But he surely heard about them and their great skill in hunting buffalo. While still in his early twenties, Taoyateduta came to know much of the Dakota nation. Wherever he traveled, he was almost certain to find someone who was a distant relative. If he didn't, there was a sure remedy: he could marry into the band.

Taoyateduta could have found a bride in a Mdewakanton village. As a messenger, Taoyateduta met young women from all the villages of his band. But in the early 1830s, he went to the Wahpekutes, not the Mdewakantons, for his bride. And unlike his father, who had brought his wife Miniokadawin home to Kaposia, Taoyateduta stayed with the Wahpekutes after he married.

When Seth Eastman, who was stationed at Fort Snelling, drew a scene looking down on the fort in 1846–48 (top), the river was serene. Contrast this view with one made of St. Paul's bustling levee just over ten years later, in 1859.

Certainly there wasn't much to draw him back to Kaposia. When hunters couldn't find enough muskrats or other animals to pay what they owed, traders started taking back the guns and traps they'd loaned to Cetanwakanmani's people. Without guns and traps, the people had no way to feed themselves. By 1831, they were starving. Taoyateduta's grandfather was desperate. He pleaded with Major Taliaferro to help them. "It would be better to knock us on the head," Cetanwakanmani told him, "than to starve us to death."

During the winter of 1833 and 1834, Cetanwakanmani died. His son, Wakinyantanka, took over as leader of a starving, dwindling village. Willing to try almost anything to save his people, Taoyateduta's father asked Taliaferro to help him learn to farm as the Wasicu did—with men and oxen driving a metal plow into the rich, black earth. Only a desperate man would propose such a thing, since the Dakota knew that farming was women's work.

Wakinyantanka gave plowing just one try, in the spring of 1834. Taliaferro sent a Wasicu named Samuel Pond to teach the Dakota to farm in the white man's way. Taoyateduta's father and another man from Kaposia struggled to hold onto the plow. It bucked and swayed so strongly that the two Dakota were, in Pond's words, "like men wrestling." He broke out laughing—a response Wakinyantanka didn't appreciate. Pond hadn't meant any harm, but Taoyateduta's father wasn't pleased to be laughed at by a Wasicu in front of his people.

Taoyateduta had no desire to return to a village where the men were reduced to farming. At least on Wahpekute lands there was still some game to be found. It was a good place for a young man to show his skills as a hunter and a provider. Not long after Taoyateduta chose his first wife, he married again. Having more than one wife was not uncommon among the Dakota. A good hunter like Taoyateduta could kill more game than just one wife could handle.

But Taoyateduta had more than hunting and marriage on his mind when he came to the Wahpekutes. By hunting well, he showed his skill and bravery. By marrying, he gained many new brothers and sisters and cousins. He was forming ties within the village, ties that might someday make him a leader among his adopted people.

It was a hope that didn't last. No one knows why, but in the 1830s Taoyateduta left the Wahpekutes and his two wives and their babies. When a Dakota marriage ended, the village took care of the wives and children. Taoyateduta and his former wives were free to marry again. Taoyateduta might have gone back to the Mdewakantons, but once again he turned away from his old home.

In 1836, smallpox hit many Mdewakanton villages. Many died of the disease. The Kaposia people were luckier than most. The doctor at the fort vaccinated many of the villagers, and they survived. But they were still hungry. Taliaferro was urging Wakinyantanka to sell Dakota land to the United States. In return, he said, the Great Father would give the leader food and money to help his people. Facing all of these challenges, Wakinyantanka turned to his younger sons for help. His oldest son, Taoyateduta, had left the Wahpekutes and moved out west to a place called Lac qui Parle.

Buffalo hunt, painted by Seth Eastman in 1846–48.

The Dakota had named the long, wide place on the Minnesota River *Mde Iyedan,* "the lake that talks." French traders translated the name directly, calling it *Lac qui Parle,* and English-speaking people used the French name. The most important man at Lac qui Parle was a French-Dakota named Joseph Renville. Renville was the son of a French voyageur, or traveling trader, and of a Dakota woman. Renville had married a niece of Taoyateduta's father, so Taoyateduta was related to Renville and his family. He found it easy to fit into life at Lac qui Parle.

Besides Renville's trading post, there was a village of Wahpeton and Sisseton Dakota and a sprinkling of wooden houses built by Wasicu. The whites were missionaries sent by churches in the United States. They hoped to convince the Dakota to abandon traditional ways—to stop hunting and start farming and to convert to Christianity. They also hoped to teach the Dakota to read and write.

In the mid-1830s, Taoyateduta began attending the Wasicu school. It was just a frame building with a wood stove and rough plank flooring. There was no chalkboard. But missionaries drew large letters on pieces of newspaper and tacked them up on the walls. They created a written alphabet based on the sounds in the Dakota language. Using that alphabet, they taught many Dakota to read and write. "It was not difficult," one of the missionaries recalled. "A young man has sometimes come in, proud and unwilling to be taught, but by sitting there and looking and listening to others, he has started up with the announcement, 'I am able.'"

Taoyateduta was an especially fast learner. He went to school with his relatives Lorenzo Lawrence and Paul Mazakutemani and other grown men. None of them felt awkward learning the alphabet or numbers. In fact, Taoyateduta felt so much at ease that he soon was counting the Wasicu way. Instead of saying, *"wancha, nonpa, yamne"* as he bent his fingers down one by one, he saw in his head the numbers drawn on old newspapers at the Lac qui Parle school.

For a time, Taoyateduta even went to the Lac qui Parle church. He learned about the white men's savior, Jesus Christ. The missionaries meant well, but they had so many rules. Dakota Christians—even the men—were all supposed to farm the land. Dakota Christian men had to cut their hair short and wear the odd-looking outfits of the whites instead of leggings and blankets. And Dakota Christian men could have only one wife. For Taoyateduta, becoming a Christian was impossible.

Sometime during the summer of 1838, he married the village leader's oldest daughter. She had three sisters. As the years passed, Taoyateduta convinced the leader to give him the other daughters in marriage as well. He felt that marrying sisters was a good choice. They helped each other cook the meat and treat the skins of the game he hunted. As sisters they were less likely to fight or be jealous of each other. Visitors to his lodge agreed that Taoyateduta's family was a happy one, and that Taoyateduta was a devoted husband and father—when he was home.

Taoyateduta had made a place for himself at Lac qui Parle, but he still loved to roam. Sometimes he even traveled to his childhood home, Kaposia. But in 1837, his father and other Mdewakanton leaders had signed a treaty with the United States, selling all of their land on the eastern side of the Mississippi River. Wakinyantanka and his people moved their village to the west side of the river. As soon as the Dakota left their bark lodges, white settlers rushed in to claim the land and turn the woods into farms. When Taoyateduta visited he could see the smoke rising from their chimneys and the cornstalks drying in their fields.

Many other things had changed at Kaposia. Taoyateduta's younger brothers and sisters were no longer the little children he remembered. Some were men and women with families of their own to raise.

Another big change was money. Now members of the Kaposia band gathered in the fall to receive their annuity, an annual payment agreed upon in the treaty. Because of the regular annuities—money and supplies from the United States—the Mdewakanton

Minneapolis in 1854 was still, for the most part, Dakota country.
John H. Stevens's frame house pokes out above the tepees at the
far right in this photograph.

no longer had to depend on hunting and trapping for all of their
needs. Part of their annuity was food: flour, pork, and corn. Taoyateduta's young nieces and nephews grew fat on a Wasicu diet of
meat and bread.

His brothers and cousins—all brave men—seemed unsure how
to fill their days. In the past, men proved themselves as hunters or
warriors. As game grew scarcer and scarcer each year, the men
struggled to show they were good hunters. To show their bravery
in battle, they wanted to raid Ojibwe camps to the north. But the

Indian agent and soldiers at the fort punished the Dakota and Ojibwe when they waged war. With few options left to them, many men at Kaposia turned to drinking.

The changes Taoyateduta saw at Kaposia did not make him want to return. They may, however, have given him an idea of how to earn a living. Taoyateduta was a good hunter, but even the best hunter would have had difficulty feeding a family year-round from the game near Lac qui Parle. With all he had learned about Wasicu numbers and the appeal of whiskey, Taoyateduta was ready to go into business as a trader.

Just up the Mississippi from Kaposia on the east side of the river was a Wasicu settlement called St. Paul. It was mostly a gathering of crudely built saloons, or "grog shops," as they were called then. Taoyateduta bought kegs of whiskey at those shops, loaded them into canoes, and paddled them up the Minnesota River to sell to Sisseton and Wahpeton family and friends. Some whiskey traders sold part of a keg's contents along the way, filling it up with water after each stop. Whether they were honest or not, traders brought home huge profits in ponies and buffalo hides and blankets. In the early 1840s, Taoyateduta did well enough that white traders complained he was hurting their business.

Taoyateduta couldn't have competed with the Wasicu if he hadn't been cunning. He had mastered numbers well enough that he was able to tell traders just how much he owed them. Or how much they owed him. Eventually, he even tried his hand at poker, a Wasicu card game that was all about numbers. Anyone who watched him play a game and clean out the other players was sure to steer clear of him. And anyone who hadn't seen him play poker before was sure to lose his blanket or his shirt.

When Taoyateduta traveled up the Minnesota River, gambled with soldiers at the fort, or brought game to his family at Lac qui Parle, people noticed him. A fur trader named Henry Sibley never forgot the intelligent and athletic young man he knew in the early 1840s. Taoyateduta led a winter hunt in 1841 and invited Sibley to come along. Sibley had a horse and easily followed the herd of elk they were tracking. Taoyateduta effortlessly kept pace as well—

Downtown St. Paul in 1853, at around Third and Wabasha Streets, had progressed beyond a collection of "grog shops" to include, at center, a bookstore.

running nearly thirty miles each day for almost a week over the winter snows.

With such strength and ability, Taoyateduta seemed ready to become a leader of his people. He was impatient to prove himself, to show others how strong and brave and smart he was.

CHAPTER 3

Leader of Kaposia, Speaker for the Dakota

I was only a brave then; I am a chief now.

TAOYATEDUTA, ABOUT 1846

The chief is a man of some forty five years of age & of a very determined & ambitious nature, but withall exceedingly gentle and dignified in his deportment. His face is full of intelligence when he is in conversation & his whole bearing is that of a gentleman.

FRANK MAYER, 1851

TAOYATEDUTA'S chance to lead did not come as he might have expected it. During harvesttime at Kaposia, his father had been riding in a Wasicu cart. When it hit a bump, Wakinyantanka's gun went off by accident and wounded him. Kaposia's leader knew he wouldn't last long. He called two of his sons to him and gave the oldest his instructions. Taoyateduta had been gone too long. Wakinyantanka was passing over him, choosing another son to be leader.

No one knows how quickly the news traveled up the Minnesota River to Lac qui Parle. Perhaps Taoyateduta was away on the fall

At first, when the artist Frank Mayer met Taoyateduta in 1851, the leader refused to sit for a portrait. "He declined sitting to me until he was dressed in a manner more becoming his rank," Mayer wrote. When Taoyateduta finally did sit to have sketches drawn, Mayer took notes on what the leader wore: "His headdress was peculiarly rich, a tiara or diadem of rich work rested on his forehead & a profusion of weasel tales fell from this to his back & shoulders. Two small buffalo horns emerged on either side from this mass of whiteness, & ribbons & a singular ornament of strings of buckskin tied in knots & colored gaily depended [hung] in numbers from his head to his shoulders & chest."

hunt when word arrived of his father's death and of the new leader. He waited for the spring thaw before he and his family and a group of close friends launched canoes into the river. He was returning to Kaposia to challenge his brother.

Taoyateduta's two oldest brothers were ready when he arrived. They stood with the whole village on the banks of the Mississippi as Taoyateduta's canoe floated near Kaposia. "You are not wanted here," one brother called out. "Go and live at Lac qui Parle."

Standing tall and unarmed, arms crossed over his chest, Taoyateduta called back, "Shoot then where all can see. I am not afraid and they all know it."

His brothers were brave, but Taoyateduta's challenge unnerved them. One managed to shoot, just missing Taoyateduta's chest. The lead shot passed through his overlapping forearms, shattering the bones. While his brothers fled deep into the woods, his supporters from Lac qui Parle laid Taoyateduta down in the canoe and paddled quickly to the fort. Wasicu medicine had kept the people of Kaposia safe from smallpox. Perhaps the Wasicu doctor could make Taoyateduta's arms whole again. A leader needed his hands and arms. So did a hunter and a warrior.

Inside the doctor's office a fire blazed, casting light on the saw used to take off arms and legs. Looking at Taoyateduta's wounds, the doctor explained that it was a hopeless case. Both arms had to be sawn off. Otherwise infection would spread. But Taoyateduta refused. He asked his supporters to take him back to Kaposia, to the Dakota healer there. It was a risky plan. Taoyateduta's brothers might well be planning to return and attack. His family and supporters from Lac qui Parle might not be safe at Kaposia. He, too, would need protection.

For weeks, Taoyateduta waited for the Dakota healer's herbal medicines and prayers to work. The people of Kaposia waited, too. They wondered about this man who spent so much time away from home. Finally, Taoyateduta began to recover. Although his wrist bones were shattered and he was never again able to move some of his fingers, his recovery seemed like a miracle. The people of Kaposia saw it as a sign of Taoyateduta's bravery and fitness to lead. They threw their support behind Wakinyantanka's oldest son.

Now Taoyateduta would listen to the people of Kaposia when they met in council. Now he would speak for them when the Wasicu asked for treaties. And now he would ask them and his supporters from Lac qui Parle to hunt down his two oldest brothers and kill them. Their bones, he said, should be thrown into the river. As far as Taoyateduta was concerned, they had no place on the cluster of wooden platforms on the hills above Kaposia. They did not deserve a proper Dakota burial. Taoyateduta allowed his remaining brothers to live. They were the children of his father's third wife and too young to be a threat to his power.

In the summer of 1846, Taoyateduta settled into life at Kaposia. It was a different life from the one he had known as a boy. The changes bore heavily on his mind when he cradled his newborn son, *Wowinape* (Appearing One), in his arms. Babies in Kaposia were so used to eating the annuity flour that they asked for bread and spit out the corn their mothers grew. The hills and streams on the eastern side of the Mississippi, the ones Taoyateduta had explored as a boy, were filled with Wasicu settlers. Their town of St. Paul was growing. More people than he remembered bustled around the fort. Everywhere, the Wasicu were crowding in. How could one raise a Dakota boy in such a place?

For Taoyateduta, survival depended on taking the best from the Wasicu while leaving the rest behind. So in November 1846 he asked a missionary to open a school in Kaposia. Taoyateduta thought his people needed the letters and numbers he'd learned at Lac qui Parle. While Taoyateduta couldn't stomach Christianity himself, he saw no harm in it for others. Even some of his wives had converted.

Dr. Thomas Williamson and his sister, Jane, were pleased when the young leader asked them to come to his village. But they couldn't have been happy when Taoyateduta continued to sell whiskey to other Dakota along the Minnesota River. To Taoyateduta, it made perfect sense. The government annuities did not give the Dakota enough food and money to survive. Game near Kaposia was scarcer than ever, what with white settlers hunting, too. Farming, although it suited some of his relatives from Lac qui Parle, like Lorenzo Lawrence and Paul Mazakutemani, was not for Taoyateduta. Like most Dakota, he saw farming as women's work, whether the corn was planted in small mounds of dirt or in big plowed fields.

Taoyateduta's work as a trader brought in some much-needed income. From time to time, his travels also gave him the chance to show his bravery and skill as a warrior. In 1848, he came upon a group of Ojibwe on Dakota lands. It was a hunting party, and Taoyateduta led the attack—and took away the hunters' pelts in the process.

Little Crow / Taoyateduta

While Taoyateduta traveled from St. Paul's saloons to scattered Dakota villages, he heard about changes to the east. On the other side of the St. Croix River, on land Taoyateduta had known as a child, the Wasicu were forming a state. They called the place Wisconsin. It was to be part of the United States.

One year later, in 1849, whites living west of the St. Croix in tiny settlements and towns like St. Paul formed a territory they called Minnesota. They used a Dakota word, *minisota,* meaning "whitish water." But Taoyateduta could see that they meant to make a Wasicu country of it, a place like their United States.

Dr. Thomas Williamson was an early missionary to the Dakota.

Word soon reached Taoyateduta that the new territorial governor, Alexander Ramsey, was interested in negotiating a treaty. Ramsey wanted still more Dakota lands. Taoyateduta wasn't surprised. Of all the Mdewakanton leaders, he lived closest to the Wasicu and their towns. The treaty his father had signed in 1837 gave the whites the right to settle on a slender strip of land between the St. Croix and Mississippi Rivers. But smoke from cabin fires now smudged the skies well west of the Mississippi. And more Wasicu kept coming.

In the summer of 1851, Governor Ramsey let it be known that he and other whites were ready to negotiate. Much about the negotiations made Taoyateduta uneasy. Governor Ramsey was negotiating first with the Sissetons and Wahpetons to the west of Kaposia. Taoyateduta heard from his friends at Lac qui Parle that times for these Dakota were very hard. Deer and muskrat and buffalo seemed impossible to find, and many of the people were starving. When people were hungry, they might agree to almost any deal. And if the Sissetons and Wahpetons sold their lands to the Great Father, the Mdewakantons and Wahpekutes would be hemmed in on both sides, east and west, by white settlers.

Taoyateduta made a point of traveling to Traverse des Sioux, near present-day St. Peter, on the Minnesota River to watch negotiations with the Sissetons and Wahpetons. His old acquaintance, the trader Henry Sibley, was part of the Wasicu group. Surrounded by familiar faces, Taoyateduta relaxed enough to allow a Wasicu artist named Frank Mayer to draw his portrait. But when the Wasicu and the Dakota gathered under an arbor made of freshly cut tree branches, he strained every muscle to hear and to remember the words that were spoken.

Governor Ramsey rose first and talked of the Great Father, or president, in Washington and his wishes. "He has learned," said Ramsey, "that you have broad lands up here, notwithstanding that you and your children sometimes starve in summer and freeze in winter. He has been informed that there is little or no game on these lands, and that for all your purposes as Indians, they are of little benefit to you; while he has many white children who would improve them."

Ramsey and a Washington official spoke of settling the Dakota on a strip of land along the Minnesota River. The official explained the president's wishes: "Your Great Father intends to place farmers among you when you are settled there, to teach and help you to cultivate the soil. . . . He expects, likewise, that in a few years, you will all have comfortable houses to live in; that your children will be taught to read and write as those of the white people are; that you will not only have corn in plenty, raised by yourselves, but cattle, horses, and other animals; that you will have both provisions and clothing sufficient to keep you from starving or freezing."

For the land, the Great Father would pay the Sissetons and Wah-petons over $1.6 million. Certainly all these promises sounded good, at least to those Dakota who were willing to farm. But once negotiations ended, one older Dakota, Big Curly Head, stood and spoke his mind. "You think it a great deal of money to give for this land," he said, "but you must well understand that the money will all go back to the whites again, and the country will also remain

Even after the Dakota were made to live on reservations and take up farming
in the 1850s and 1860s, women continued to do much of the farm work,
as they traditionally had.

theirs." Surely Taoyateduta and other Dakota would have agreed
that, one way or another, the Wasicu always managed to get the
best of any treaty or deal. In spite of such feelings, the Sissetons
and Wahpetons signed the treaty.

Later that month, treaty negotiations with the Mdewakantons
and Wahpekutes began in Mendota, a small trading settlement
on Mdewakanton land above the mouth of the Minnesota River.
Ramsey's offer to them was similar to that made to the western
Dakota. In return for their wooded homeland around the Mississippi and lower Minnesota Rivers, Ramsey promised money and
"a comfortable home . . . for you and your children, in all time to

Taoyateduta attended treaty negotiations between the U.S. government and the Sissetons and Wahpetons at Traverse des Sioux in 1851. He later spoke for the Mdewakanton Dakota at negotiations for a separate treaty at Mendota.

come, between the Yellow Medicine and Red Wood rivers." The eastern Dakota would have a reservation on prairie lands just east of the Sisseton and Wahpeton reservation.

On the first day of negotiations, Wabasha was spokesman for the Dakota, but no decisions were made. As another leader noted, "Our habits are different from those of the whites, and when we have anything to consider, it takes us a long time." Over the next few days, one decision was made: Taoyateduta would speak for the Dakota. Perhaps he had convinced the others that he understood the Wasicu well, that he was unafraid of their numbers and would only agree to a fair price, or that he was brave enough to remind the Wasicu of promises left unfilled from the treaty his father signed in 1837.

On July 31, he rose. *"Fathers,"* he said, "These chiefs and soldiers, and others who sit here, have something they wish to say to you, and I am going to speak it. There are chiefs here who are older than myself, and I would rather they had spoken it; but they have put it upon me, and I feel as if my mouth was tied. These chiefs ... speak of some money that is due them; it was mentioned the other day to Gov. Ramsey; and we spoke about it last fall; but we have not yet seen the money. We desire to have the money laid down to us. It is money due on the old treaty, and I think it should be paid; and we do not want to talk on the subject of a new treaty, until it is all paid."

Ramsey tried to change the subject, but Taoyateduta wouldn't budge. "We will talk of nothing else but that money, if it is until next spring," he answered. The Dakota had another complaint. The reservation land set aside for them was "too much prairie." Taoyateduta explained that the Mdewakanton were people of the woods. The Sissetons and Wahpetons might like living on the tall-grass prairie, but how could the Mdewakanton live in such a place? Any reservation had to include some wooded lands.

Ramsey and the government official made vague promises about the money owed under the old treaty. And they agreed to extend the reservation a bit farther. Not as far as Taoyateduta had asked, but far enough. On August 5, 1851, the eastern Dakota were ready to sign the agreement. The man they chose to sign first could write his own name in his own language: Taoyateduta.

CHAPTER 4

The Politician

Little Crow was a gifted, ready and eloquent speaker, and in council was always ready to answer any demand made by the government. . . . His appeals in these addresses to the government and to the Great Spirit that justice be done to his people, with his rugged eloquence, the lighting up of his countenance, the graceful pose of his person, and the expressive gestures, presented a scene wonderfully dramatic. He was possessed of a remarkably retentive memory, enabling him to state accurately promises made years before to these Indians by government officials and to give the exact amount of money owing them, to the dollar and cent.

DR. ASA DANIELS, WHO MET TAOYATEDUTA IN 1854

TAOYATEDUTA hoped his people could survive on annuity payments and meat and furs from the Big Woods north and east of the reservations. Other Dakota were not as optimistic. The treaties were in trouble almost from the start. The U.S. Congress in Washington wasn't eager to give the Dakota reservations. Why, after all, couldn't the Dakota simply move west, beyond Minnesota Territory? Taoyateduta could have told them why. Minnesota was his home and the home of the Dakota for as long as they could remember. The Mdewakantons in particular were woodland people. The western plains could never be their home.

Wabasha spoke the words of many Mdewakantons. "There is one thing more which our great father can do," he said, "that is, gather us all together on the prairie and surround us with soldiers and shoot us down." Governor Ramsey and others finally got the Dakota their reservations by going straight to President Franklin Pierce. But the trouble didn't end there.

White settlers moved onto Dakota lands while the ink on the treaties was still drying—and well before Congress ratified the two documents. As Taoyateduta put it that spring, "White settlers came in and showered down their houses all over our country. We did not really know, whether this country any longer belonged to us or not." Because the Mdewakantons and Wahpekutes lived closest to white settlements in the east, they were most troubled by squatters, settlers living illegally on their land.

The Sissetons and Wahpetons had their own troubles. In 1851 at Traverse des Sioux, leaders were asked to sign a second paper. Most thought it was a copy of the treaty. Instead, it gave traders a large part of their first payment under the treaty. Most Dakota owed money to the traders and were glad to pay it back if they could. But they wanted to do so on their own terms. They needed the money to cover the costs of moving to the reservations. When the leaders discovered how they had been tricked, they were angry and disgusted.

Tempers flared in 1853 when officials in Minnesota began urging the Dakota to move to the reservations. What exactly, many Dakota wondered, were they moving to? Good roads linking the reservations to food and supplies in St. Paul didn't yet exist. The Minnesota River couldn't be relied upon as a "road" during the freezing winters.

People in Kaposia did not begin packing for the move to their new reservation, called Redwood Agency, until the next year. It was hard to leave a land they had known so long. If they were to move, they wanted to have their leader with them. In the spring of 1854, Taoyateduta had been busy visiting Washington, D.C., as a guest of the United States. Taoyateduta returned to Kaposia full of stories of a fantastic iron machine called a train that traveled faster than any horse, of cities that filled the landscape as far as the eye could see, and of the vast distances he covered. He also brought back a suit of Wasicu clothes. Although the suit was hot and scratchy, Taoyateduta wore it from time to time at his new home.

When Taoyateduta arrived at Redwood Agency in the summer of 1854, he was one of the most important and influential Dakota leaders. At Redwood, he was constantly in motion. He supervised government workers as they built him a frame house. He watched over officials who gave out the annuity payment in the late summer or early fall. He visited trading posts and stores at Redwood, talking about events in Minnesota Territory and the United States. He also traveled to the reservation of his Sisseton and Wahpeton relatives. The headquarters for that reservation, known as Yellow Medicine Agency, were a day's horseback ride away.

Asa Daniels, who met Taoyateduta that summer, was impressed by the Mdewakanton leader. "He was," the reservation doctor remembered later, "of a nervous temperament, restless and active,

Ta-oyate-duta.
Little Crow.

Thomas Waterman Wood painted this portrait of Taoyateduta in about 1860,
showing him in a mix of Indian and white clothes.

intelligent, of strong personality, of great physical vigor, and vainly confident of his own superiority and that of his people."

Taoyateduta did what he could to make his people comfortable. But the annuity payment in 1854 was late. The food—thousands of pounds of flour, pork, and corn stored in wooden barrels—was nearly spoiled by water and heat by the time it reached western Minnesota. And there wasn't much of it. That fall, a missionary at Yellow Medicine wrote that the Dakota were "half-starved" *after* the payment and food distribution were made.

At first, most Dakota lived on the reservations only for the weeks leading up to the annuity payment each summer or fall. For the rest of the year, they went back to their traditional homes. They fished, hunted and trapped game, and planted corn in their old fields wherever whites had not yet settled.

Some Dakota planted crops on reservation lands. These Dakota were mainly Christians. Many followed missionary friends to settlements at Yellow Medicine. Dr. Williamson formed a settlement called Pezutazi [Pah-zshu-tah-zi], where Taoyateduta's father-in-law, the old leader from Lac qui Parle, tended his fields. Another missionary, Stephen Riggs, created what he called the Hazelwood Republic. Many of Taoyateduta's old friends, including Lorenzo Lawrence and Paul Mazakutemani, joined Riggs. They cut their hair, wore Wasicu clothes, and worked their own fields. At each settlement, missionaries and government employees encouraged the Dakota to store their harvests in root cellars to have food to last the winter. But in the Dakota tradition of giving, farmers frequently shared their crops with hunters.

THE POLITICIAN

In the mid-1850s at Yellow Medicine and Redwood, "Farmer" Dakota were few. Even on the reservation, Taoyateduta and most of his people managed to continue living a traditional Dakota life. Villagers settled together within the reservations, although they often left to hunt. Annuities, though poor, usually kept them

Stephen Riggs founded the Christian mission at Hazelwood, where Dakota were taught how to farm and how to read and write.

from starving in the lean times when fish and game were hard to find in the Big Woods. But white settlers were quickly moving closer to the reservations. More and more were clearing trees to make fields on traditional Dakota hunting lands. Even bigger changes for the Dakota came in March 1857. Word reached Redwood and Yellow Medicine of killings to the south. Near a place called Spirit Lake, in Iowa, a Wahpekute warrior named Inkpaduta had attacked white settlers.

White Minnesotans had a hard time making distinctions among Indians. If Dakota in Iowa were killing settlers, then all Dakota were enemies. Hunting parties from Redwood and Yellow Medicine were attacked by whites. The government threatened to withhold the annuity that year if the Dakota at the reservations could not catch and punish Inkpaduta.

Taoyateduta and other Dakota leaders were in a dangerous situation. It was no good telling the Wasicu that Inkpaduta was acting on his own. Whites thought all Indians were the same. The newspaper in Red Wing proclaimed, "We have plenty of young men who would like no better fun than a good Indian hunt."

Hoping to keep the peace and to save the annuity, Taoyateduta volunteered to lead a party of men in search of Inkpaduta. He asked Dakota from both reservations to go along with him. He even got his father-in-law to leave his fields and join the search. The men never found Inkpaduta, but their efforts convinced government officials to pay the annuity that summer. They could not, however, convince Minnesota's white settlers to forget their fears. After Spirit Lake, reservation officials did all they could to convince the Dakota to stay at Redwood and Yellow Medicine year-round.

If any of the whites had asked, Taoyateduta could have told them it was a bad idea, that the Mdewakanton needed the freedom to hunt in the woods and to live in traditional ways. But no one asked. The whites were sure the plan would work—as long as Dakota men became farmers. In the fall of 1857, Joseph Brown was appointed Indian agent. Brown was white but had married one of Taoyateduta's relatives, Susan Frenier. Susan's husband thought farming was the key to Dakota success. As Indian agent he had the means to make sure that the small group of Farmer Dakota grew, even if it meant tearing the Dakota people apart.

Starting in 1857, Brown began rewarding Farmer Dakota for farming and for doing extra work. More traditional, "Blanket" Dakota received only the annuity payment and food each summer. Brown had more to offer farmers who grew crops and helped on government projects—such as building a stone warehouse at Redwood. These Dakota received clothing and tools and livestock worth much, much more than the annuity.

Taoyateduta opposed Brown's new policies. For a time, the leader went around "declaring that early death would be visited upon [the Dakota] if they forsook the ways of their fathers." But no one listened to Taoyateduta. All around him at Redwood, Dakota men were sporting new haircuts and stiff Wasicu clothes. Taoyateduta could hardly blame them. The annuity payments were skimpier each year. With officials asking that no one leave the reservations to hunt, the Dakota had few ways to support

A delegation of Dakota leaders traveled to Washington, D.C., in 1858 to negotiate
a new treaty. Taoyateduta, not pictured here, demanded payments that had
been promised in previous treaties, but government officials refused to listen.

themselves apart from farming. Finally Taoyateduta decided to
hold his tongue. He would give the farmers a chance, "hoping it
might result in good for his people."

Perhaps he also thought some good might come from a new
treaty. Late in 1857, Taoyateduta and many other leaders were invited
to Washington to negotiate a treaty. Most were hopeful that they
would have a chance to talk with government officials. Taoyateduta

brought a list of complaints and intended to get to the bottom of each one. When negotiations began in the spring of 1858, he talked first of money that had been promised to his people under the 1837 and 1851 treaties. Somehow, he noted, all the money hadn't made its way to Redwood in Minnesota. Perhaps, he joked, the money had spilled out of the wagons like so much whiskey from a leaky keg. "If I were to give you an account of all the money that was spilled," he told officials, "it would take all night."

But government officials weren't interested in hearing complaints. Agent Brown was planning to allot each Dakota family eighty acres on which to farm and live. To do this, he would need only about half of the land at Redwood and Yellow Medicine. The United States was asking the Dakota to sell half of their reservations—all on the north side of the Minnesota River.

Government officials wanted the Dakota to sign the treaty quickly. With each new question Taoyateduta raised, he was faced with more documents that seemed to contradict agreements he remembered clearly from the past. Finally, Taoyateduta said in disgust, "It appears you are getting papers all around me, so that, after a while I will have nothing left." He and other Dakota leaders eventually signed the treaty, but they weren't happy about it.

While touring the city, Taoyateduta met former Indian agent Lawrence Taliaferro. "We have lost confidence in the promises of our Great Father, and his people," the leader told Taliaferro, "bad men have nearly destroyed us." Taoyateduta seemed discouraged. He spoke with great sadness of men who were forcing his people to live like the Wasicu. His sadness would only grow.

Taoyateduta, known as Little Crow, in about 1858.

CHAPTER 5

Stranger in His Own Land

It came without their asking for it—a totally different way of life, far reaching in its influence, awful in its power, insistent in its demands. It came like a flood that nothing could stay. All in a day, it seemed, it had roiled the peacefulness of the Dakotas' lives, confused their minds, and given them but one choice—to conform to it, or else! And this it could force them to do because, by its very presence, it was even then making their old way no longer feasible.

ELLA DELORIA, YANKTON DAKOTA HISTORIAN AND
ANTHROPOLOGIST, 1944

They were advised to turn their attention to agriculture, but . . . they were fed like paupers in a poor-house.

SAMUEL POND, 1902

TAOYATEDUTA returned in the summer of 1858 to a changed reservation. All summer long, Brown and the Farmer Dakota had been busy building houses. The banging of their hammers rang out in the air. Other houses were popping up along the eastern and southern edges of the reservation—sometimes even on reservation lands. These homes belonged to a new wave of settlers, many of them immigrants from Germany. They didn't speak

55

English well, and few learned Dakota. The Dakota called them "Bad Speakers." Taoyateduta called many of them squatters, but officials did nothing to stop those who were building their farms on Dakota lands.

The leader's frustrations grew when the payment due under the new treaty was delayed. When young Dakota men pressed Taoyateduta for details about what the treaty had to offer, he could only point to a few presents. Congress took its time ratifying the treaty. Then all the money owed to the Mdewakantons went instead to traders to pay off debts. Taoyateduta had nothing to show for months of negotiations. His people felt he had let them down. As one Mdewakanton later put it, "Little Crow made the greatest mistake of his life when he signed this agreement."

In the spring of 1859, the Mdewakanton held an election for their spokesman. This person would speak for all the Mdewakanton villages now gathered at Redwood Agency. Taoyateduta lost. His world seemed to be crumbling around him. As more Mdewakantons joined the Farmer Dakota and built frame homes, Taoyateduta's village shrank. Many of his friends and relatives seemed eager to join the ranks of the farmers. Taoyateduta's influence grew smaller by the day.

By the winter of 1861, the former leader of the Mdewakantons was begging for food from settlers in the Big Woods. Cutworms had destroyed most of the corn crop at Redwood and Yellow Medicine. Even Farmer Dakota were going hungry that winter. Taoyateduta knew the Indian agent wouldn't open his warehouse to Blanket

Dakota. He and his villagers spent the winter in the woods, doing their best not to starve.

Taoyateduta may have hoped that the newly elected president, Abraham Lincoln, would be generous to the Dakota. The leader saw changes brought by the new administration as soon as he reached Redwood that spring. But the changes weren't for the better. In place of Joseph Brown, Lincoln appointed a new agent, Thomas J. Galbraith, a Republican. If Taoyateduta had disliked Brown's policies, he had never disliked the man. But Thomas Galbraith was a hard man to like. Stubborn in his ways and unwilling to see things from another person's point of view, Galbraith was also inexperienced. He'd had few dealings with Indians before. But he was eager to turn Dakota men into farmers.

In 1861, Galbraith made it known that only those Dakota who stayed year-round on the reservations would be receiving annuities that summer. Even though all the treaties said otherwise, under Galbraith's policy simply being Dakota no longer gave one the right to an annuity payment. Galbraith's policy could not help but divide the Dakota.

The worst trouble seemed to be at Yellow Medicine. There, fewer Dakota had become farmers. Many still hunted buffalo and lived most of the year on the plains. They came to Yellow Medicine for the annuity payment each summer and then left. But soon some were staying on the reservation. They stayed just long enough to try to scare Farmer Dakota. Some killed oxen used to plow fields.

Some tore down fences. Others insisted that Farmer Dakota share food stored in their root cellars.

At Redwood, farmers were also harassed, but things seemed calmer on the surface. Since Taoyateduta had returned to the reservation in 1858, each spring he had asked government farmers to plow fields for his wives to farm. He and his family lived in a two-story wooden cabin, though he still kept a tepee in the yard. Taoyateduta might have seemed content, but he foresaw a dark future for his people.

Up to now, most Blanket Dakota had managed to avoid starvation on their annuity and whatever they could earn by hunting and trapping. When game was hard to find, or while they awaited

Dozens of brick houses were built by the U.S. government as it tried to convince Indian men to farm. Many of the Dakota, Taoyateduta included, built tepees outside their brick houses and lived there rather than in the Wasicu structures.

the arrival of the annuity each summer, they bought food on credit at the traders' stores. Most bought more than they could pay back. Most were hopelessly in debt.

Sarah Wakefield, whose husband took a job as doctor at Yellow Medicine in 1861, recalled the scene between traders and Dakota at that summer's annuity payment:

> Indians would buy on credit, promising to pay at the time of payment. They have no way of keeping accounts, so the traders have their own way at the time of payment. All the Indians are counted, every person giving his name, each band by themselves. At the time of payment they are called by name from the window to receive their money (which . . . was only nine dollars to each person). As soon as they receive it the Traders surround them, saying, you owe me so much for flour. Another says you owe me so much for sugar, &c., and the Indian gives it all up, never knowing whether it is right or not. Many Indians pay before the payment with furs, still they are caught up by these Traders, and very seldom a man passes away with his money. I saw one poor fellow one day swallow his money. I wondered he did not choke to death, but he said "They will not have mine, for I do not owe them."

Taoyateduta could still remember a time when traders like Henry Sibley had been his friends. He believed that the new traders were too harsh in their dealings with the Dakota. They seemed only interested in money, not friendship. They didn't understand the Dakota way of looking at debts. The Dakota thought, as one hunter put it, "that the traders ought not to be too hard on them about the payments, but do as the Indians did among one another, and put off the payment until they were better able to make it."

Annuities, or yearly payments of food supplies and money, were made to
Indians who had signed over land to white settlement, illustrated in this
wood engraving from 1871.

By the spring of 1862, many Dakota who kept to traditional
ways were starving. Many, too, would ask the traders to extend
more credit than they could possibly repay, well before the annuity
came. Taoyateduta himself was taking a second look at some of
the Wasicu ways he had always scorned. That summer, he began
attending the mission church on Sundays. The minister there was
hopeful that Taoyateduta would become a Christian. Taoyateduta
also began digging a cellar at the site of the new brick house that
was to be built for him as leader. He had not yet become a farmer.
As usual, his wives tended fields plowed by reservation workers.
He had not yet cut his hair. But he sometimes wore his fancy
Wasicu suit and white gloves.

Watching Taoyateduta that summer, reservation officials might
have thought the former leader was finally warming up to the
idea of becoming a farmer. But when traders cut off credit to
most Blanket Dakota that summer and the annuity payment was
late, young Dakota men talked with Taoyateduta. He listened

sympathetically to their complaints, pleased that the young men thought he could help. But there was nothing he could do.

At Yellow Medicine, some Dakota held a protest when the annuity was late. Others, hungry and impatient, broke into the warehouse. Lieutenant Timothy Sheehan from nearby Fort Ridgely, just down the Minnesota River from Redwood, managed to keep the break-in from turning into a war. He also persuaded the Dakota to talk with the agent and traders. Taoyateduta was there. He listened to agent Galbraith, who insisted that the food in the warehouse shouldn't be given out until the annuity money arrived. When pressed, Galbraith admitted that he didn't know when the money might come. It was weeks late already, and the U.S. government had bigger problems to deal with. Hundreds of miles from Yellow Medicine and Redwood, southern and northern states were fighting each other in the Civil War. Who knew how long it might take the government to send the annuity?

Taoyateduta had a suggestion. "We have no food, but here are these stores, filled with food," he said, motioning toward the trading posts. Then he turned to Galbraith. "We ask that you, the agent, make some arrangement by which we can get food from the stores." Taoyateduta knew Galbraith could pay the traders back from the annuity money when it arrived. To force a decision, the leader added, "We may take our own way to keep from starving. When men are hungry they help themselves."

But Galbraith couldn't make up his mind. He asked the traders what they thought. Finally Andrew Myrick, who had already closed his store to Blanket Dakota that August, rose to leave. On his way out, he said, "So far as I am concerned, if they are hungry, let them eat grass." Taoyateduta heard the trader add another comment—that if they didn't like grass, they should eat "their own dung."

Myrick's remarks stung. The trader's main concern was getting paid—not making sure that the Dakota had food to eat. But Taoyateduta and many other Dakota knew that Myrick wasn't too far from the truth. That August, as thousands of Dakota waited for the annuity payment, all their hunting and trapping and fishing scoured the land around the reservations of food. As one woman remembered, when some Dakota were given dry corn, they "were so near starvation that they ate it raw like cattle." Eating uncooked grains leads to diarrhea. A whole village with diarrhea could create a desperate situation. "They could not wait to cook it," the woman went on, "and it affected them in such a manner that they were obliged to remove their camp to a clean spot of earth." Those Dakota were lucky. Others tried to live on green raspberries, wild turnips, and marsh grasses.

When Lieutenant Sheehan's commander, Captain John Marsh, arrived at Yellow Medicine, he realized that Galbraith and the traders weren't going to hand over food unless they were forced. He ordered Galbraith to open the warehouse. For a while, at least, Dakota at Yellow Medicine wouldn't starve.

Before leaving Yellow Medicine, Taoyateduta asked Galbraith to do the same at Redwood. After all, his people were hungry, too. Galbraith agreed. But when he came to the reservation on August 15, Galbraith did nothing to ease the hunger there. Instead, he was looking for Dakota men and men of both Dakota and white back-

"An Indian, having plenty of ducks, went one day to Beaver Creek and wished to exchange them for potatoes. He said, when telling me of it, that his ducks were fresh and good; that they took them and gave him potatoes that a hog could not eat, they were so soft. Now, this is the way many befriended the Indians; gave them what they could not eat themselves. This is the way the Indians have been treated for years."
Sarah Wakefield, 1864

grounds. He was asking any men he could find to join the Union army and fight in the distant Civil War.

Galbraith soon left with a group of recruits, headed for St. Paul. The agent probably did not know that the Dakota at Redwood were recruiting soldiers of their own. They had formed a soldiers' lodge. Usually formed to keep order on long hunting trips, a soldiers' lodge was also used to keep order during war. In the summer of 1862, the soldiers' lodge was a place for young Dakota men—angry with traders, upset with white settlers, and hungry for food—to gather. And it was just the place where a group of young hunters would go when trouble arose between the Dakota and the settlers.

CHAPTER 6

A Cast-off Leader Goes to War

[A]ll they cared for was food—it was not our lives; and if all these Indians had been properly fed and otherwise treated like human beings, how many, very many innocent lives might have been spared.

SARAH WAKEFIELD, 1864

Ta-o-ya-te-du-ta is not a coward: he will die with you.

TAOYATEDUTA, 1862

ON AUGUST 17, 1862, a few young Dakota hunters went to the cabin of a settler, Robinson Jones, near Acton, Minnesota. There are several stories to explain what happened next. One story says the men wanted to buy whiskey from Jones, but he refused to sell them any. He'd sold them whiskey before, and his refusal angered them. Another story says the men found a hen's nest along the fence near Jones's house. One man took eggs from the nest and asked for a pot to cook them in. When the woman of the house heard about the stolen eggs, she shoved the Dakota man right out of her cabin. Someone in the hunting party accused the man of being a coward. He answered by calling out to his friends, "come with me and show some of your bravery." Then he marched right back to the cabin. Whatever the reason, Dakota hunters killed five white settlers at the cabin and elsewhere near Acton.

That night, the hunters arrived at the soldiers' lodge at Redwood. When members of the lodge learned what had happened, they knew that all Dakota people would be affected. The U.S. government would surely refuse to pay the annuity. Officials would demand that the killers be turned over. And they would no doubt take money—probably a very large sum—from the annuity to compensate the families of the dead settlers. The Dakota could not afford to lose money. They were starving. Most owed all of their annuity payment to the traders. Members of the soldiers' lodge grew angrier and angrier—too angry to consider working out a deal or turning in their friends. They were ready for war. All they needed was a leader who could unite the Dakota people.

Taoyateduta was asleep when the men arrived. On the ground floor of his house was a low, sofa-like shelf built into a wall. There, Taoyateduta and his family slept. And there, in the big ground-floor room, the members of the soldiers' lodge crowded around the former leader's bed just before dawn.

When the men told Taoyateduta what had happened and asked him to lead them in a war, he flatly refused. He said they were fools— fools to fight the Wasicu and fools to ask him. After all, he wasn't the speaker for the Mdewakanton. They should ask Traveling Hail, who had won the election.

But the men persisted. Someone argued that "the whites must be pretty hard up for men to fight in the South, or they would not come so far out on the frontier and take half-breeds or anything

In this photograph from 1862, Taoyateduta covers his black suit with an Indian blanket.

to help them." Surely the Great Father was too busy to counter a Dakota attack.

Taoyateduta reminded warriors of the vast cities he had seen on his trips to Washington, D.C. He tried to argue them out of waging such a hopeless war. But his arguments fell on deaf ears.

The men taunted him. Had Taoyateduta grown old and tired? Was he no better than a farmer, hiding food in his cellar? Was he a coward?

"*Ta-o-ya-te-du-ta* is not a coward," he answered hotly, "and he is not a fool." No Dakota warrior could stand by quietly when called a coward. Taoyateduta launched into a speech that his oldest son, Wowinape, remembered perfectly, even years later:

Braves, you are like little children; you know not what you are doing. You are full of the white man's *devil-water* [rum]. You are like dogs in the Hot Moon when they run mad and snap at their own shadows. We are only little herds of buffaloes left scattered; the great herds that once covered the prairies are no more. See!—the white men are like the locusts when they fly so thick that the whole sky is a snowstorm. You may kill one—two—ten; yes as many as the leaves in the forest yonder, and their brothers will not miss them. Kill one—two—ten, and ten times ten will come to kill you. Count your fingers all day long and white men with guns in their hands will come faster than you can count.

Yes; they fight among themselves—away off. Do you hear the thunder of their big guns? No; it would take you two moons to run down to where they are fighting, and all the way your path would be among white soldiers as thick as tamaracks in the swamps of the Ojibways. Yes; they fight among themselves, but if you strike at them they will all turn on you and devour you and

A CAST-OFF LEADER GOES TO WAR

your women and little children just as the locusts in their time fall
on the trees and devour all the leaves in one day. You are fools. You
cannot see the face of your chief; your eyes are full of smoke. You
cannot hear his voice; your ears are full of roaring waters. Braves,
you are little children—you are fools. You will die like the rabbits
when the hungry wolves hunt them in the Hard Moon.

But the old leader couldn't end his speech without replying to
the men's taunts. Was he really too old and tired to lead? Was he a
coward? No, he said firmly, *"Ta-o-ya-te-du-ta* is not a coward: he will
die with you."

Taoyateduta had been raised to value bravery, but it took more
than the fear of seeming a coward to drive him into battle. With a
name like Taoyateduta—His Red Nation—he had always seemed
destined to lead, impatient to show off his greatness. Yet his
own people had cast him aside. Here was a chance to lead again.
Taoyateduta wasn't willing to wait for another chance. He would
lead a war against the Wasicu, even a hopeless war.

Over the years, Taoyateduta had gained a reputation as a warrior
against the Ojibwe. Now his enemy was different, but his strategy
was the same. The Dakota would strike quickly, killing the whites
at Redwood. They would raid the great stone warehouse for food
and guns and powder. Then they would attack nearby settlements
and the fort. If they could take Fort Ridgely and the largest
Wasicu town in the region, New Ulm, they would continue east to
the Mississippi River, pushing white settlers in front of them. All
this was possible if the warriors acted quickly—before soldiers arrived from the east.

The first attack went well for the Dakota. On the morning of August 18, Dakota men surrounded the warehouse and trading posts at Redwood. They quickly killed about twenty people, including the trader Myrick, whose mouth they stuffed with grass. But almost as soon as the killing ended, the warriors' organization began to fall apart. Many began looting houses and trading posts. Men wore sunbonnets stolen from chests of women's clothes. They tied gold watches to their ankles as decorations. Many drank whiskey from the traders' stores. They gorged themselves on food until they were too full to do anything but sleep. Others captured enemies of the Dakota who hadn't managed to get away from the agencies and nearby settlements. They would hold these captives prisoner as long as they were at war.

When Taoyateduta tried to attack Fort Ridgely, he couldn't find enough warriors to join him. Quick attacks, aided by the element of surprise, were not to be. Taoyateduta wanted to attack the fort early and quickly, but his men preferred to loot. Until he could gain the ear of his warriors, he could not be the strong leader he wanted to be.

People gathered around Taoyateduta's house. The once shrinking village grew into a bustling town overnight. Dakota set up tepees and lodges, waiting to find out what was going on. Many had been startled by the war. One Dakota girl remembered thinking that the gunfire at Redwood must be from an attack of Ojibwe, or Chippewa, Indians. "Hurry," the girl's mother had cried. "The Chippewa must be here."

Other people gathered around Taoyateduta's house were cap-

A Cast-off Leader Goes to War

tives—some white, some of both Dakota and white backgrounds. All were confused and scared. Warriors forced captives and Farmer Dakota to wear traditional clothes. Taoyateduta sometimes seemed annoyed by the captives and the need to feed and clothe them. One white woman who had been generous to Taoyateduta before the war asked the leader for some food. "He became very cross,"

Susan Brown and her children were captured early in the war, and because she was related to Taoyateduta he protected her family.

she remembered. "Pointing to a sack of flour he said: 'There is flour; if you are hungry, make yourself some bread,' and then he left the house."

Taoyateduta may have viewed captives as bargaining chips. If he needed to make peace, or if any of his people were captured, then he could use the captive women and children to make the whites listen to him. Taoyateduta did what he could to keep young warriors from threatening the captives. And he made some of the captives comfortable in his own home.

Susan Brown, the wife of the former agent, stayed with Taoyateduta after she was captured. Susan was related to many important Sissetons and Wahpetons. Taoyateduta hoped to have their help in the war, so he made sure Susan had everything she might need. He also explained to her why he was fighting against the Wasicu. As her son Samuel recalled, Taoyateduta "said to her that he wanted her to know all about the troubles that have so suddenly come upon his people. . . . He said in substance that his young men had started to massacre; that he at first opposed the movement with all his might, but when he saw he could not stop it he joined them in their madness against his better judgment, but now did not regret it and was never more in earnest in his life."

On August 20, Taoyateduta had finally gathered enough warriors to attack Fort Ridgely. The Dakota fought the whites just as they would have ambushed Ojibwe in the forest, firing their weapons from behind trees or clumps of grass. White soldiers were not used to this strategy. As one warrior put it, "The white men stood up and exposed themselves at first, but at last they learned to keep

Wamditanka, or "Big Eagle," fought with Taoyateduta in the war of 1862.
Wamditanka described the fighting at the battle of Birch Coulee this way:
"Owing to the white men's way of fighting they lost many men. Owing to the
Indians' way of fighting they lost but few."

quiet." Although the whites suffered more casualties than the Dakota, they did not give up the fort.

Taoyateduta returned for another attack on August 22. This time four hundred Sissetons and Wahpetons joined the fight. Even with these reinforcements, the Dakota were forced to retreat. The same thing happened when Taoyateduta led two attacks on New Ulm. The Dakota burned most of the town, but the whites held out.

By late August, Taoyateduta was complaining to Susan Brown of a headache. At first he joked that it happened when he hit his head dodging a cannonball at the fort. But then he went on more seriously. "I am worried—," he told her, "ammunition is giving out. We could of course use clubs, sticks and stones, and drive the whites out of the country, but . . . that would take a long time."

Time was running out for the Dakota. Taoyateduta had gotten word that Henry Sibley was leading a large army. The army was on its way to Redwood to fight the Dakota. Taoyateduta urged his people to move north to Yellow Medicine. He hoped to find support there among his Sisseton friends and relatives. Instead, Paul Mazakutemani, his relative from Lac qui Parle, was leading a group of Farmer Dakota—and Blanket Dakota—who opposed the war. Little Paul, as he was known, was just as skilled a speaker as Taoyateduta. Even some of the leader's own warriors had to agree when Little Paul warned, "No one who fights with the white people ever becomes rich, or remains two days in one place, but is always fleeing and starving."

Little Paul urged the Dakota to make peace with the whites and return the captives. But for the moment, the Dakota seemed to be gaining the edge in the war. The Dakota lost relatively few men in the fighting, yet they had killed more than five hundred whites. Most of the dead were settlers. Some were women and children. Taoyateduta warned his warriors that the Wasicu would never forgive the deaths of women and children. But some civilian deaths could not be avoided in war.

On August 31, the leader and his warriors held a council on the prairie. With their blankets wrapped around them, they talked of their plans late into the night. One group, led by Taoyateduta, would go into the Big Woods. They would attack settlements. Another group would head toward New Ulm.

On the way to New Ulm, however, warriors discovered a group of white soldiers camped for the night near a creek called Birch Coulee. When the Dakota saw the soldiers' campsite, they knew they had to attack. The white men had chosen a spot that was nearly impossible to defend. Over two days, Dakota warriors shot at soldiers and their horses, killing all of the latter. They took breaks to drink water from the creek while the white soldiers suffered from terrible thirst. And they ate food prepared by their wives at campfires just out of range of the soldiers' guns. The fighting only stopped when more soldiers came to save those few still trapped at Birch Coulee.

Meanwhile, Taoyateduta attacked settlements in the Big Woods. Many whites fled to the east. When he arrived back at Yellow Medicine on September 7, Taoyateduta hoped his victories would gain him support. But that support didn't come. He wanted to move his warriors and their captives farther north, but some Sissetons

resisted. "I live by the white man . . . and by the buffalo," said one
Sisseton. "I fear that you are going to annihilate all these for me,
therefore you shall not advance north of here."

Yet Taoyateduta did move north, slowly, in a long and noisy train
of people in wagons, on horseback, and on foot. His attention was

Alexander Ramsey was governor of Minnesota at the outbreak of the war.
Speaking before the state legislature on September 9, 1862, he said, "The Sioux
[Dakota] Indians of Minnesota must be exterminated or forever driven
beyond the borders of the state."

A CAST-OFF LEADER GOES TO WAR

Members of the Riggs family, missionaries to the Dakota,
and others rest on the prairie during their escape from the war of 1862.

turning toward plans for another battle. By September 21, Sibley
had reached an area near Yellow Medicine called Wood Lake.
Taoyateduta wanted to attack the sleeping soldiers at night. Others
argued that a morning attack when the troops reached Yellow
Medicine would work best. At about the same time, Taoyateduta
sent Sibley a note, saying "I want to know from you as a friend
what way that I can make peace for my people."

But a warrior can't make peace and war at the same time. Sibley
didn't reply to the note. Taoyateduta and his men began their attack.
Early on September 23, when Sibley's army was leaving camp for
Yellow Medicine, a small group of soldiers was sent ahead to dig
potatoes. They surprised Dakota warriors, waiting to ambush the

whole army. The battle didn't go at all as planned. Sibley's soldiers turned cannons on the Dakota before they could complete their attack. Taoyateduta and his warriors retreated.

By the time Taoyateduta returned to camp, he knew the war was lost. Farmer Dakota and others friendly to the whites had stolen away most of the captives. Taoyateduta's last bargaining chips were gone. Susan Brown's son Samuel described the leader as "despondent" and "heart broken." Taoyateduta's voice was full of disappointment when he summed up how the war had gone: "Seven hundred picked warriors whipped by cowardly whites. . . . Better run away and scatter over the plains like buffalo and wolves."

After this last speech to his people, Taoyateduta told his wives and supporters to get ready to travel. A long, cold winter lay ahead. Early on the morning of September 24, Taoyateduta rode over the prairie and left his red nation behind. Coming to a rise, he turned his pony around for one last look. "We shall never go back there," he said.

CHAPTER 7

A Place in History

Our course then is plain.

The Sioux [Dakota] Indians of Minnesota must be exterminated or forever driven beyond the borders of the state.

GOVERNOR ALEXANDER RAMSEY, SEPTEMBER 9, 1862

They desire to possess the whole world.

For thirty years they were trying to entice us to sell them our land. Finally the outbreak gave them all, and we have been driven away from our beautiful country.

A DAKOTA REMEMBERING THE WORDS OF HIS UNCLE ABOUT THE WAR

TAOYATEDUTA LED a small band out onto the plains. He still hoped, or said he hoped, to find allies. Perhaps the Yankton and Yanktonai or the Tetons to the west would join him in the war. Perhaps the British to the north in Canada would help him. After all, his ancestors had helped the British fight the Americans in 1812. But Taoyateduta had no success in gaining allies. He had only slightly more success finding food and shelter for his party.

By early 1863 word must have reached him about the fate of the Dakota warriors who stayed behind, confident in Sibley's promises not to harm those who had not killed women and children. In makeshift military courts, where dozens of Dakota men were tried in a day, hundreds were sentenced to death for having fought in the war. President Lincoln eventually reduced the number of those under death sentences. But nearly three hundred went to prison. And just a day after Christians celebrated the birth of their savior Jesus, thirty-eight warriors were hanged at once. It was the largest mass execution in U.S. history.

That spring found Taoyateduta at Devils Lake, in what is now North Dakota. From there, he planned one last raid into Minnesota. He said he wanted to steal horses so that each of his children would have a pony—a necessary tool when living on the plains and hunting buffalo. Most of their animals had died during the harsh winter.

Wowinape and a few others joined Taoyateduta in a raid that June. But the group didn't stay together long. The leader was soon alone with his oldest son. The two were picking raspberries one evening as the first stars shone in the sky. They were near Hutchinson, Minnesota. It was July 3, 1863. A settler and his son happened upon the two Dakota. And, as any Minnesota settler would likely have done so soon after the war, they opened fire. Taoyateduta grabbed a gun and shot back. One settler shot again, this time hitting his mark.

Taoyateduta knew his injuries were fatal. He asked Wowinape for a drink of water. He seemed happy to be going to the land of his fathers. He didn't fight death. Wowinape took his father's medals and medicine bag and put clean moccasins on Taoyateduta's feet.

His father would need good moccasins on his journey into the afterlife. Then Wowinape made his way alone to Devils Lake.

Many have wondered why Taoyateduta made that last trip to Minnesota. Was he hoping to see Sibley, his old friend, and ask for a peaceful surrender? Was he seeking his own death by putting

Taoyateduta prepared his oldest son, Wowinape, "the Appearing One," to succeed him as chief. As Dr. Asa Daniels recalled, "His oldest son . . . was his great pride. When government officials were to be present at an important council, this son, dressed in the most elaborate manner, with embroidered garments, ribbon decorations, and two silver medals on his neck, was led into the assemblage and presented as his son and successor."

himself in the path of a bullet? Or was he simply trying to provide his children with ponies?

Whatever his reason, the world he left behind was as different from the world of his boyhood as any two places could be. Since 1858, the land itself had been known as the state of Minnesota. Most of the inhabitants were bent on making sure that none of the Dakota people lived there. Taoyateduta's people, his red nation, were scattering in many directions.

Those who surrendered or were later captured found themselves in prison or on desolate reservations far from home. Hundreds died from hunger and disease. Those who survived carried with them stories too horrible to tell. Dakota who fled to the plains joined with other Indian bands. Many eventually found homes on reservations in the Dakotas and Nebraska. Those who traveled north settled on reserves in Canada.

The land was new to them. The way of life was hard. Returning to Minnesota seemed impossible. Only death waited for them there. Scattered as they were, relatives lost touch with relatives. On reservations, hunters and warriors became farmers. In fighting their war against the Americans, the Dakota lost nearly everything. But the Dakota did not die. Some who supported the U.S. government stayed on. In the years after the war, small groups returned. By the late 1800s, Dakota communities were reforming, back in Minnesota.

Americans celebrated Independence Day on the day following Taoyateduta's death. Some of the people of Hutchinson brought his body to town and left it on the main street. Boys put firecrackers

A Place in History

On the river bottom below Fort Snelling, thousands of Dakota were held by the U.S. government during the winter of 1862. Gabriel Renville recalled that illness broke out among the captives. "It seemed doubtful," he said, "whether a person would be alive in the morning."

in his ears and nose. Before long, he had been scalped and his head removed. The rest of his body was thrown in the town dump. By the time the people of Minnesota realized that the dead Indian might be the man they called Little Crow, the horrible devil who'd led a war against them, the body was just a pile of bones. From the strangely shaped lower arms, shattered by gunshot and then healed nearly twenty years before, the body was finally identified.

The settler who killed him was given five hundred dollars by the state. Taoyeduta's scalp was, for many years, displayed at the state historical society. Only in 1971 were his remains finally gathered and put to rest. A grandson asked for the right to bury Taoyateduta near the family home in South Dakota.

So for a time, Taoyateduta himself was scattered to the four winds. And for many years, his role in the war with the Americans was greatly misunderstood. Was he a devil who drove his people into a bloody war against women and children? Or was he a man hoping to find some way to survive in a changing world? He had gone to church at the mission on Sunday, the day before the war began, dressed in a suit of Wasicu clothes. He had gone to bed that night hopeful, perhaps, that the annuity would arrive soon. Hopeful that his people might not starve that year, that summer. He had gone to bed a tired man, a cast-off leader of a divided people.

He awoke into a whirling storm of fear and anger. It was a morning that would forever change his world, yet the changes had begun long before. They had begun when the first boatload of white soldiers arrived to build a fort just up the river from Kaposia, while a young Dakota boy played in the woods.

GLOSSARY

allot	to assign a portion, as of land
annuity	yearly payment, as those agreed upon in a treaty
Blanket Dakota	Dakota who held on to traditional ways
cede	to give up possession
council	gathering in which people discuss questions and work to reach agreement
Farmer Dakota	Dakota who chose to cultivate the land as white people did
fast	to eat nothing, usually in preparation for a religious ceremony
Great Father	name for the U.S. president
missionary	one who carries religious teachings to others
muskrat	an aquatic rodent whose fur was traded by the Dakota
ratify	to approve and make valid, as in a treaty
reinforcements	additional soldiers or weapons that strengthen a force
reservation	land set aside, often by treaty
smallpox	an often fatal infectious disease that causes chills, fever, headache, backache, and pimples or "pox"
squatter	one who builds on another's land without permission
vaccinate	to infect with a mild form of a disease so as to prevent later, more severe illness
voyageur	a traveling trader

Dakota Names and Words

Canpasa wi (Chan-pa-sha wi) — the moon when chokecherries ripen (July)

Cetanwakanmani (Che-tan-wa-kan-ma-ni) — Charging Hawk

Chaska (Cha-ska) — first-born son

Istawicayazan wi (Ishta-wi-cha-ya-zan wi) — the moon of sore eyes (March)

Kapozia (Ka-po-zi-a) — traveling light

Maga okada wi (Ma-ga o-ka-da wi) — the moon when geese lay eggs (April)

Mde Iyedan (Mde I-ye-dan) — the lake that talks (Lac qui Parle)

Michinkshi (Mi-chin-kshi) — my son

Miniokadawin (Mini-o-ka-da-win) — Woman Planting in Water

minisota (mi-ni-sho-ta) — whitish water

miniwakan (mi-ni-wa-kan) — spirit water (whiskey)

Psinhnaketu wi (Psin-hna-ke-tu wi) — the moon for laying up rice to dry (September)

shunktokeca (shunk-to-ke-cha) — wolf

Tahecapsun wi (Ta-he-cha-pshun wi) — the moon when deer shed horns (December)

Takiyuha wi (Ta-ki-yu-ha wi) — the moon when deer mate (November)

DAKOTA WORDS

Taoyateduta (Ta-o-ya-te-du-ta)   His Red Nation or People

Wakinyantanka (Wa-kin-yan-tan-ka)   Big Thunder

wancha, nonpa, yamne
   (wan-cha, non-pa, ya-mni)   one, two, three

Wasicu (Wa-shi-chu)   white people

Wasuton wi (Wa-su-ton wi)   the moon for harvesting ripe corn (August)

Watopapi wi (Wa-to-pa-pi wi)   the rowing moon, the moon when rivers and streams thaw (April)

Wazupi wi (Wa-zhu-pi wi)   rice drying moon (October)

Wazustecasa wi
   (Wa-zhu-shte-ca-sha wi)   the moon when strawberries are red and corn is hoed (June)

Wicata wi (Wi-cha-ta wi)   raccoon moon (February)

Witehi wi (Wi-te-hi wi)   hard moon (January)

Wowinape (Wo-wi-na-pe)   Appearing One

Wozupi wi (Wo-zhu-pi wi)   the moon for planting corn (May)

CHRONOLOGY

1805   Lieutenant Zebulon Montgomery Pike of the U.S. Army buys 100,000 acres of land from the Mdewakanton Dakota Indians.

1810   Taoyateduta is born at about this time. He is the first son of Wakinyantanka and Miniokadawin and the grandson of Cetanwakanmani, leader of the Kaposia band of Mdewakanton Dakota, who live near present-day St. Paul, Minn.

1820   The U.S. Army begins building Fort Snelling at the mouth of the Minnesota River.

early 1830s   Taoyateduta lives among the Wahpekute Dakota, where he is said to have married two daughters of a band leader and to have had two sons and a daughter.

winter of 1833–34   Cetanwakanmani dies, and Wakinyantanka becomes leader of the Kaposia band.

1837   In the fall, a delegation of Dakota leaders, including Taoyateduta's father, goes to Washington to sign a treaty ceding lands east of the Mississippi River and all its islands.

Beginning at about this time, Taoyateduta lives for several years at Lac qui Parle, among the Wahpeton and Sisseton Dakota.

1838   Taoyateduta marries the oldest daughter of Inyangmani, the Wahpeton Dakota leader at Lac qui Parle. He later marries her three sisters.

1840s   Taoyateduta sells whiskey along the Minnesota River.

1845   Wakinyantanka dies from an accidental gunshot wound. One of his younger sons, Taoyateduta's half-brother, becomes leader of the Kaposia band.

CHRONOLOGY

1846   In May, Taoyateduta returns to Kaposia to claim his father's title as leader. Two of Taoyateduta's half-brothers, including the current leader, are killed so that Taoyateduta can assume his role as leader.

In November, Taoyateduta invites white Christian missionary workers Dr. Thomas Williamson and his sister, Jane, to Kaposia to start a church and school.

1849   Minnesota Territory is created. Territorial governor Alexander Ramsey reaches St. Paul, capital of the new territory.

1851   At Traverse des Sioux, north of present-day St. Peter, Minn., the Dakota sign treaties ceding nearly all their lands in Minnesota Territory. Under the agreement, the Dakota receive a cash payment and an annuity from the U.S. government. The treaty requires the Dakota to live on two small reservations—the Yellow Medicine or Upper Agency and the Redwood or Lower Agency—on the Minnesota River.

1853-54   Late payment and the poor quality and quantity of food included in the annuities discourage the Dakota from staying on or near the reservations.

1858   In the spring, Taoyateduta and other Dakota leaders go to Washington, where they are presented with a treaty requesting half of their lands, those on the north side of the Minnesota River.

In May, Minnesota is admitted as the thirty-second state.

1861   After the election of Abraham Lincoln as president, Thomas Galbraith is appointed the new Indian agent for Yellow Medicine and Redwood Agencies.

1862   After Dakota men kill five settlers near Acton, Minn., on August 17, Taoyateduta agrees to lead the Dakota in a war against whites, attacking first Yellow Medicine and Redwood, then New Ulm, Fort Ridgely, and other locations in southwest Minnesota.

After the Battle of Wood Lake, on September 23, and the retreat of Taoyateduta and many other Dakota warriors to the west, the war is over.

CHRONOLOGY

On the day after Christmas, the military commission charged with prosecuting Dakota involved in the war executes thirty-eight Dakota at Mankato, Minn. Nearly all other Dakota in Minnesota are imprisoned or forced to leave the state and live on reservations farther west.

1863   On July 3, while picking berries near Hutchinson, Minn., Taoyateduta is fatally shot by a white farmer.

1971   Taoyateduta's descendants successfully gain control of his remains from the Minnesota Historical Society and give him his final burial.

SOURCE NOTES

v "Now what have we? . . ." : quote from *Minnesota Pioneer*, May 27, 1852.

4 A more accurate translation into English of *Taoyateduta* might be "His Red People" rather than "His Red Nation." Nation, in the modern sense of a politically organized group, doesn't do a good job of describing the bonds between the Dakota, Nakota, and Lakota people, who were organized in seven "council fires"—the Mdewakanton, to which Taoyateduta belonged, as well as the Sisseton, Wahpeton, Wahpekute, Yankton, Yanktonai, and Teton. But to many modern readers, *nation* suggests a federation of people more clearly than does *people*, hence the translation used in this book.

5 "The half-grown boys & the dogs . . ." : Frank Blackwell Mayer, 200.

5 "They told me that their nation . . ." : Mary H. Eastman, *Dahcotah*, 13.

12 "follow the example of the *shunktokeca* . . ." : Charles Eastman, *Indian Boyhood*, 54.

14 "Give food! . . ." : Ella C. Deloria, 29.

16 The Yankton Dakota scholar Ella C. Deloria translated the term *Wasicu* to mean "ingenious, clever, cunning, supernaturally efficient" (Deloria, *Speaking of Indians*, 46). But another translation is "taker of the fat," suggesting greed. The word carries both meanings; however, nowhere in it is the meaning "white," a common modern translation. Charles Eastman, a Dakota born shortly before the Dakota War of 1862, translated Wasicu as simply "the rich." But his uncle's description of white men and their ways suggests a broader meaning: "They are wonderful people. They have divided the day into hours, like the moons of the year. In fact, they measure everything. Not one of them would let so much as a turnip go from his field unless he received full value for it" (Eastman, *Indian Boyhood*, 283).

91

16 "for a song" : Gary Clayton Anderson, *Kinsmen of Another Kind*, 82.

17 "a steady, generous and independent Indian" : Thomas Forsyth, 217.

17 "must not think that anything bad was intended . . ." : Forsyth, 202.

18 "My father I take you by the hand" : quoted in Gary Clayton Anderson, *Little Crow*, 25.

21 "The village at Lac-qui-parle . . ." : Stephen R. Riggs, *Mary and I*, 32.

24 "It would be better to knock us on the head . . ." : quoted in Anderson, *Little Crow*, 28.

24 "like men wrestling" : Samuel W. Pond, 9.

27 "It was not difficult . . ." : Riggs, *Mary and I*, 38–39.

33 "I was only a brave then . . ." : quoted in Return I. Holcombe, 184.

33 "The chief is a man of some forty five years of age . . ." : Mayer, 125.

35 "You are not wanted here . . ." : Holcombe, 181.

35 "Shoot then where all can see . . ." : Holcombe, 182.

40 "He has learned . . ." : quoted in W. G. Le Duc, 52–53.

40 "Your Great Father intends to place . . ." : Le Duc, 54–55.

40 "You think it is a great deal of money . . ." : Le Duc, 66.

41 "a comfortable home . . ." : Le Duc, 72.

42 "Our habits are different . . ." : Le Duc, 76.

43 "*Fathers,* These chiefs and soldiers . . ." : Le Duc, 77.

43 "We will talk of nothing else . . ." Le Duc, 78.

43 "too much prairie" : Le Duc, 83.

44 "Little Crow was a gifted, ready and eloquent speaker . . ." : Dr. Asa W. Daniels, 517.

45 "There is one thing more . . ." : quoted in S. R. Riggs to S. B. Treat,

NOTES

31 July 1852, American Board of Commissioners for Foreign Missions Papers.

45   "White settlers came in . . ." : quoted in *Minnesota Pioneer*, 27 May 1852.

46   "He was of a nervous temperament . . ." : Daniels, 514.

48   "half-starved" : Mary Ann Longley Riggs, 212.

50   "We have plenty of young men . . ." : quoted in Meyer, 102.

51   "declaring that early death . . ." : Daniels, 524.

52   "hoping it might result . . ." Daniels, 524.

53   "If I were to give you an account . . ." : quoted in Anderson, *Little Crow*, 101.

53   "It appears you are getting papers all around me . . ." : Anderson, *Little Crow*, 103.

53   "We have lost confidence . . ." : quoted in Lawrence Taliaferro, 253.

55   "It came without their asking for it . . ." : Deloria, 46.

55   "They were advised . . ." : Pond, 185.

56   "Little Crow made the greatest mistake . . ." : Charles Eastman, *Indian Heroes*, 50.

59   "Indians would buy on credit . . ." : Sarah Wakefield, 7.

59   "that the traders ought not to be too hard . . ." : Gary Clayton Anderson with Alan R. Woolworth, 24.

61   "We have no food . . ." : quoted in Winifred Barton, 48.

62   "So far as I am concerned . . ." : Barton, 49.

62   "their own dung" : *Executive Documents of the State of Minnesota for the Year 1862*, 444.

62   Several sources quote trader Andrew Myrick as saying that the Dakota should "eat grass," but it is not clear exactly when and in what context Myrick said these words. He may have restated the same point several times in different contexts during those tense weeks in August 1862.

NOTES

62 "were so near starvation . . ." : Wakefield, 9–10.

65 "All they cared for was food . . ." : Wakefield, 8.

65 *Ta-o-ya-te-du-ta* is not a coward . . ." : Anderson and Woolworth, 42.

65 "come with me and show some of your bravery" : Thomas A. Robertson Papers, 41.

66 "the whites must be pretty hard up . . ." : Anderson and Woolworth, 26.

68 *Ta-o-ya-te-du-ta* is not a coward . . ." : Anderson and Woolworth, 40.

68 "Braves, you are like little children . . ." : Anderson and Woolworth, 40–42.

69 *Ta-o-ya-te-du-ta* is not a coward . . ." : Anderson and Woolworth, 42.

70 "Hurry! The Chippewa must be here" : Anderson and Woolworth, 53.

71 "He became very cross . . ." : Helen M. Tarble, 31–32.

72 "said to her that he wanted her to know . . ." : Anderson and Woolworth, 131.

72 "The white men stood up . . ." : Anderson and Woolworth, 150.

74 "I am worried— . . ." : Anderson and Woolworth, 173.

74 "No one who fights with the white people . . ." Anderson and Woolworth, 196.

76 "I live by the white man . . ." : Anderson and Woolworth, 200.

77 "I want to know from you as a friend . . ." : *Executive Documents*, 445.

78 "despondent" and "heart broken" : Anderson and Woolworth, 222.

78 "Seven hundred picked warriors . . ." : Anderson and Woolworth, 223.

78 "We shall never go back there" : quoted in *St. Paul Pioneer Press*, 24 October 1897.

79 "Our course then is plain . . ." : *Executive Documents*, 12.

79 "They desire to possess the whole world . . ." : Eastman, *Indian Boyhood*, 282–83.

BIBLIOGRAPHY

Books

Anderson, Gary Clayton. *Kinsmen of Another Kind: Dakota-White Relations in the Upper Mississippi Valley, 1650–1862.* St. Paul, Minn.: Minnesota Historical Society Press, 1997.

Anderson, Gary Clayton. *Little Crow: Spokesman for the Sioux.* St. Paul, Minn.: Minnesota Historical Society Press, 1986.

Anderson, Gary Clayton, editor, with Alan R. Woolworth. *Through Dakota Eyes: Narrative Accounts of the Minnesota Indian War of 1862.* St. Paul, Minn.: Minnesota Historical Society Press, 1988.

Barton, Winifred W. *John P. Williamson: A Brother to the Sioux.* Chicago: Fleming H. Revell Company, 1919.

Black Thunder, Elijah, Norma Johnson, Larry O'Connor, and Muriel Pronovost. *Ehanna Woyakapi: History and Culture of the Sisseton-Wahpeton Sioux Tribe of South Dakota.* Sisseton, S.Dak.: Sisseton-Wahpeton Tribe, 1975.

Carley, Kenneth. *The Dakota War of 1862: Minnesota's Other Civil War.* 1976. Reprint, St. Paul, Minn.: Minnesota Historical Society Press, 2001.

Curtiss-Wedge, Franklyn. *The History of Renville County, Minnesota.* Chicago: H. C. Cooper Jr. & Co., 1916.

Deloria, Ella C. *Speaking of Indians.* 1944. Reprint, Vermillion, S. Dak.: Dakota Books, 1992.

Eastman, Charles. *Indian Boyhood.* With illustrations by E. L. Blumenschien. 1902. Reprint, Williamstown, Mass.: Corner House Publishers, 1975.

Eastman, Charles. *Indian Heroes and Great Chieftains.* 1918. Reprint, Lincoln, Nebr.: University of Nebraska Press, 1991.

Eastman, Mary H. *The American Aboriginal Portfolio.* Philadelphia: Lippincott, Grambo and Company, 1853.

Eastman, Mary H. *Dahcotah: or, Life and Legends of the Sioux around Fort Snelling.* 1849. Reprint, Afton, Minn.: Afton Historical Society Press, 1995.

Executive Documents of the State of Minnesota for the Year 1862. St. Paul, Minn.: Wm. R. Marshall, State Printer, 1863.

BIBLIOGRAPHY

Forsyth, Thomas. "Journal of a Voyage from St. Louis to the Falls of St. Anthony, in 1819." In *Report and Collections of the State Historical Society of Wisconsin, For the Years of 1869, 1870, 1871, and 1872.* Vol. 6. Madison, Wis.: Atwood & Culver, State Printers, Journal Block, 1872, pp. 188–219.

Holcombe, Return I. *Minnesota in Three Centuries, 1655–1908.* Vol. 2. Mankato, Minn.: Publishing Society of Minnesota, 1908.

Le Duc, W[illiam] G. *Minnesota Year Book for 1852.* St. Paul, Minn.: W[illiam] G. Le Duc, 1852.

Mayer, Frank Blackwell. *With Pen and Pencil on the Frontier in 1851: The Diary and Sketches of Frank Blackwell Mayer.* Edited by Bertha L. Heilbron. 1932. Reprint, St. Paul, Minn.: Minnesota Historical Society, 1986.

Meyer, Roy W. *History of the Santee Sioux: United States Indian Policy on Trial.* Rev. ed. Lincoln, Nebr.: University of Nebraska Press, 1993.

Pond, Samuel W. *The Dakota or Sioux in Minnesota, As They Were in 1834.* 1908. Reprint, St. Paul, Minn.: Minnesota Historical Society Press, 1986.

Riggs, Mary Ann Longley. *A Small Bit of Bread and Butter: Letters from the Dakota Territory, 1832–1869.* Edited by Maida Leonard Riggs. South Deerfield, Mass.: Ash Grove Press, 1996.

Riggs, Stephen R. *A Dakota-English Dictionary.* Edited by James Owen Dorsey. 1890. Reprint, St. Paul, Minn.: Minnesota Historical Society, 1992.

Riggs, Stephen R. *Mary and I. Forty Years with the Sioux.* 1880. Reprint, Williamstown, Mass.: Corner House Publishers, 1971.

Schoolcraft, Henry, editor. *Information Respecting the History, Condition and Prospects of the Indian Tribes of the United States.* Philadelphia: Lippincott, Grambo and Company, 1852, 1853, and 1854. (See volumes 2:168–99, 3:225–46, and 4:59–72 for entries on the Dakota by Philander Prescott.)

Spector, Janet. *What This Awl Means: Feminist Archaeology at a Wahpeton Dakota Village.* St. Paul, Minn.: Minnesota Historical Society Press, 1993.

Tarble, Helen M. *The Story of My Capture and Escape during the Minnesota Indian Massacre of 1862.* St. Paul, Minn.: The Abbott Printing Company, 1904.

Upham, Warren. *Minnesota Place Names: A Geographical Encyclopedia.* Third Edition. St. Paul, Minn.: Minnesota Historical Society Press, 2001.

Wakefield, Sarah. *Six Weeks in the Sioux Tepees: A Narrative of Indian Captivity.* Shakopee, Minn.: Argus Book and Job Printing Office, 1864.

BIBLIOGRAPHY

Wall, Oscar Garrett. *Recollections of the Sioux Massacre.* Lake City, Minn.: Home Printery, 1908.

Journal Articles

Anderson, Gary Clayton. "Myrick's Insult: A Fresh Look at Myth and Reality." *Minnesota History* 48 (Spring 1983): 198-206.

Daniels, Dr. Asa W. "Reminiscences of Little Crow." *Collections of the Minnesota Historical Society* 12 (1905-8): 513-30.

Lamare-Piquot, F. V. "A French Naturalist in Minnesota, 1846." *Minnesota History* 6 (September 1925): 270-77.

Long, Major Stephen H. "Voyage in a Six-Oared Skiff to the Falls of St. Anthony in 1817." *Collections of the Minnesota Historical Society* 2 (1889): 7-87.

Miller, Frances. "Glimpses of Kaposia—the Village of Little Crow." *Over the Years* (Dakota County, Minn., Historical Society) 26:3 (November 1986): 1-11.

Taliaferro, Major Lawrence. "Auto-Biography of Maj. Lawrence Taliaferro." *Minnesota Collections* 6 (1894): 189-255.

Trenerry, Walter N. "The Shooting of Little Crow: Heroism or Murder?" *Minnesota History* 38 (September 1962): 150-53.

Williamson, John P. "Removal of the Sioux Indians from Minnesota." Edited by Frances H. Relf. *Minnesota History Bulletin* 2 (May 1918): 420-25.

Newspaper Sources

Haga, Chuck. "Another burial for Dakota leader." *Minneapolis Star Tribune,* 16 July 2000, pp. B1, 7.

Minnesota Pioneer, 27 September 1849 and 27 May 1852.

St. Paul Pioneer Press, 24 October 1897.

St. Peter (Minn.) Tribune, 19 August 1863.

Spavin, Don. "Little Crow: Dacotah Chief Finds Peace At Last." *St. Paul Pioneer Press,* 7 November 1971, pp. 7-9, 18-19.

Manuscripts

American Board of Commissioners for Foreign Missions. Papers. Typescript letters. Riggs to Treat, 31 July 1852; Williamson to Treat, 18 November

BIBLIOGRAPHY

1859; Williamson to Treat, 17 October 1862. Copies in Minnesota Historical Society Collections.

Robertson, Thomas A. Papers. Typescript memoir. Minnesota Historical Society.

Williams, John Fletcher. Papers. "Little Crow." Undated note. Minnesota Historical Society.

Videotapes

Dakota Conflict. St. Paul, Minn.: KTCA, 1993.

The Dakota Exile. St. Paul, Minn.: KTCA, 1996.

Websites

"The Dakota Conflict of 1862." Mankato, Minn.: Dakota Meadows Middle School. http://www.isd77.k12.mn.us/schools/dakota/conflict/history.htm
This website, created by middle-school students, provides a broad overview of the Dakota War, including a time line and articles relating to a variety of topics, such as the hangings of thirty-eight Dakota warriors after the war.

"Dakota Curriculum Project." http://www.dakotacurriculum.com/
This website provides lesson plans for learning about Dakota language and culture and includes audio files of the pronunciation of many Dakota words.

"Minnesota Historic Sites: Lower Sioux Agency." St. Paul, Minn.: Minnesota Historical Society. http://www.mnhs.org/places/sites/lsa/index.html
This web page provides background information on the Lower Sioux, or Redwood, Agency, where Taoyateduta led his first attack in the Dakota War of 1862. Links lead to a page on the Birch Coulee battlefield site, located on the other side of the Minnesota River.

"Minnesota's Uncivil War." St. Paul, Minn.: Minnesota Public Radio. http://news.mpr.org/features/200209/23_steilm_1862-m/
This archive page from a September 26, 2002, radio report on the Dakota War of 1862 includes audio clips, images from the war, and links to related topics.

INDEX

INDEX

INDEX

PICTURE CREDITS